Hollywood Film Acting

Hollywood Film Acting

Theodore Noose

South Brunswick and New York: A. S. Barnes and Company
London: Thomas Yoseloff Ltd

A. S. Barnes and Co., Inc.
Cranbury, New Jersey 08512

Thomas Yoseloff Ltd
Magdalen House
136-148 Tooley Street
London, SE1 2TT, England

Library of Congress Cataloging in Publication Data

Noose, Theodore, 1930–
  Hollywood film acting.

  Includes index.
  1. Moving-picture acting. 2. Acting for television.
3. Moving-pictures—United States. I. Title.
PN1995.N66   791.43'028   78–69633
ISBN 0–498–02207–2

PRINTED IN THE UNITED STATES OF AMERICA

Contents

Acknowledgments

I should like to express my thanks to the Leo Burnett Advertising Agency, Ted Schule, Producer of the Leo Burnett Advertising Agency; Helen Espie, Acting and Voice Coach; Roger Helfond, of the W/H/J Talent Agency; Sandra Joseph, of the W/H/J Talent Agency; Larry Brody, Producer, Supervising Writer, Colombia Pictures; Stu Berg, Director; Steve Poster, Cameraman; Chester L. Midgen, National Executive Secretary, SAG; and David O. Tytherleigh, Assistant Executive Secretary, AFTRA. I want to thank all other producers, directors, casting directors, agents, actors, and actresses who have contributed their views, knowledge, and experience toward the subject of this book.

Foreword

The great majority of professional talent in Hollywood are most likely in between jobs, that is, unemployed at the moment. This fact of life is an awesome responsibility to deal with by the dedicated professional, and use of his time and energies must be self-motivated if one is to remain in the mainstream of professional talent in the motion picture and television industry.

Mr. Noose has written a guideline for the beginner from his own experiences in dealing with the great amount of time most actors find on their hands in pursuit of their careers. He has found wherever their innate, individual depth of artistic talents may lie, must be motivated and self-directed much like a prospering businessman. The professional actor is one who conducts himself in a manner allowing his or her talents to emerge fully for us of other walks of life to enjoy and learn from the experience of audience participation in all the mediums in which actors perform.

I believe the talent pool in Hollywood is of greater depth than at any other time in our history. Actors who keep their life-style geared to improving their talents by all the means of self-improvement available are the performers without fear of the competition and who remain healthy in mind and spirit. A confidence in the knowledge of your craft becomes a way of life and fosters the confidence that is essential in those individuals in the industry who may employ your talents.

We who make this industry move are the professionals with individual talents wearing the hats of producers, directors, actors, casting directors, writers, agents, film editors, etc., all working with the tools of our respective crafts, and how well we use and care for these tools is our personal success and fulfillment.

I believe individual talents come in all forms and sizes in all walks of life, and no individual can or has the right to measure your talents at any given time unless you are offering those talents for hire, and then you must be prepared. In Hollywood, there can be a hundred and one reasons why you did not land the role, but it should never be because you have not done your homework. The setting of your goals, the striving for perfection, demanding the best of yourself, a total commitment, is up to you, and you will find that the best measuring stick will be your own gratification. Jack Nicklaus measures his talents with no one. Isaac Stern measures with no one, and Sir Alec Guinness measures with no one. They simply get on with demanding the very best of themselves. Certainly they need the counsel and experience of others, but they stand alone, win or lose, in the performance and ownership of their talents.

Mr. Noose has written a comprehensive guideline that can help channel time and energies in a positive direction for the actor entering the Hollywood experience. It is concise and straight-forward and gives an insight that not only can be of value to the actor, but that also can be appreciated by anyone with the slightest curiosity about the actor's responsibilities in the film industry.

Roger T. Heldfond
Co-Owner
Wormser, Heldfond & Joseph, Inc.

Introduction

Simply stated, this book is about becoming a film and television actor. What is the difference between an actor and a film actor? That is a valid question. There is a whole world of difference, differences such as: out of context scenes, immediate demands, no time for rehearsal, one-day parts—the list goes on and on. This book is about an approach that can be used in solving the problems that those differences create. This whole approach is dedicated to having you, the aspiring film actor, develop the tools that are absolutely essential to film acting. This technique is set down to exactly the way you will work on the set. It will be explained to you in the language that is used on the set, so that you are not entering into a totally unfamiliar world when and if you begin to work in films.

The difference in the demands placed on an actor began when the use of film first appeared as entertainment. Audiences were at first entertained by the mere fact that there was motion. But as the filmmakers began to realize the potential of this toy, they began to experiment and to develop the individual films to something more involved than motion alone. Techniques in the use of films were developed. Lighting was improved so that the images on the screen were something more than general outlines of figures moving about. Camera techniques and lenses were developed that brought the image closer or farther on the screen as the filmmaker desired. Soon the filmmakers sought to tell a story on film. The first stories were simple, merely expressions that led to a conclusion. That, too, began to evolve. The filmmakers added emotion and feeling to their stories. For that they had to turn to the only source available, the stage. There, on the stage, they had actors, people who could display the feelings and emotions that the stories demanded. So the filmmakers put the stories on film in the way in which they would have done it on the stage. The actors acted out their parts as they would have on the stage. They played to the person in the last row.

Then, not long after the first stories were shown, the creative filmmakers began to apply the techniques that had been developed for their stories. These techniques demanded that the actors who were performing develop different styles of their own. Gradually the filmmakers demanded more and more from the actor that was unique and different from the stage. Film began to formulate a whole different industry. It drifted farther and farther away from the stage manner of storytelling. On stage the actor would tell the audience and persuade the audience of the story within a fixed, lighted framework. Films could take the viewer from one location to another in the twinkle of an eye. Stage had the performer a small remote figure. Film could bring the performer to the screen in such close proximity that the viewer could see the blink of an eye. The director could use the expressions of the actor as an exclamation point for the emotion within a scene. He could film the actor from different angles to achieve different sensations in his audience. All of these different ways that the filmmaker had to stimulate the viewer was additional demands that the actor had placed on him. No longer was the actor to take a story from beginning to end and play his role. Now he would be interrupted in the middle of the story and told to repeat a certain line or display a certain emotion.

Films had evolved, and within this evolution there arose many different disciplines. Each discipline has its members on a production. Each member is involved in his own contribution to the overall film. Each member will appreciate less of the other disciplines than of his own. But each contributes to filmmaking: the cameraman, the sound man, the lighting man, and all the others. There are so many that I cannot name them all here. The actor must work with all of these people. Because they, too, are interested in making a film, and a good one too.

Many people enter into acting with predetermined ideas of what acting is all about. To clear away some doubts and to establish a common denominator, let us understand that your job as an actor is to convince the audience of the truth of what is happening to you. Now this sounds simple, and it is, except that how you do it is what makes you special and unique. This is what separates you from the competing talent. You will have to remain an individual personality, yet you must adapt yourself to new and unfamiliar characteristics in the roles you will be playing.

As a stage actor you had certain privileges that the film actor does not. They include: meeting other members of the cast, discussing the roles and their relationship to one another, ample time for rehearsal, and the development of a comradeship that borders on "family." All this aids in releasing a lot of pent up energy and in developing the character you are to play. But what happens when you are called upon to play a role in two or three scenes in a film that will be shot in two days? You were auditioned for the role of a retired Army colonel, but you were hired to play the role of a doctor! The script is sent to you, and you receive your work call, but you do not know who is to do the scene with you. All you will know is what is in the script and where you report. When you get there you had better be ready to work. When you arrive on that set you may be asked if you know your lines, and then again you may not be. But either way, you better know them. You may have a line reading for the director, then again you may not. You may be introduced to other members of the cast, then again you may not. Are you getting the idea of the differences? All of those privileges that were yours for the stage show have disappeared from the moment you auditioned for a film.

The description of the film job was given to show the conditions you work under in Hollywood. I know that in many parts of the country film acting is taken on a much more casual level from the audition to the actual filming. But let me assure you, more often than not you will work under conditions that I have described. Furthermore, if you can function on a "hot set" under demanding conditions, you will work anywhere that films are made. Not only will you work, but you will get a reputation of being a professional, and that, my friend, will serve you well. Production people, cast and crew, admire a professional. In the film industry, when an actor earns their admiration, it is almost a guarantee of future work.

Industry people admire a professional actor for a very selfish reason. There is nothing esoteric in their attitude. On the contrary, it is pure and simple business. The professional film actor does not cost the production company any extra money. Films are made with feeling and heart, from all concerned, producers, directors, production people, cast, and crew. But it all comes down to money. Everyone on the set is getting paid, and many of those people are getting paid very well. They receive high salaries because of their knowledge and ability, and if an actor slows down the scenes or the shooting, than he is costing the producer a great deal of money—money through time. This, in turn, reflects on the director, the producer, and another, as yet unmentioned, person, the casting director. So you can see how an otherwise excellent actor can go to Hollywood and ruin a potentially good career by being unfamiliar with the demands that will be placed on him.

Many actors who read this will say, "Hell, I know that!" They probably do. However, can they produce when the time comes to produce? They can if the knowledge and experience they have acquired can be recalled for a specific reaction or emotion to be given without rehearsal with another actor. The point is that most of us, if not all of us, in the business have heard actors say, "I couldn't get it across because the other actor didn't give me anything!" That is useless conversation in the film industry. An actor does his own work. He must react within his character regardless of how the other actor plays his part. If the director thinks that the other actor should put more reaction into his role, then he will tell him to do so. An actor is not in a position to judge another actor's performance. He must consider that the other actor may be giving the scene exactly what he believes is needed in relation to the film. The versatility of the film actor is a quality demanded by director. The director does not have time to teach versatility to an actor. That is the actor's own responsibility.

Speaking of directors! They are the men whom you never mention, if the film you have done comes out well. If, on the other hand, it does not, you blame it on him. His is a tremendous responsibility. He is usually the first one on the set and the last one to leave. When a director hires an actor, it is because he expects that actor to give something more than the basic requirements. When you read for a director, he will determine your qualifications for the role. But he expects that you will bring something to the role that will be interesting.

When you arrive on the set for work, the director expects that you have done your homework in regard to having a full characterization. The director will expect this from you whether it is one scene and one page or ten scenes and twenty pages. He does not want to tell you how the role will be played, he tells you what he wants and needs for that scene. He then expects that you will put life into that role. If you do, he will love you for it, although most directors express their pleasure with your work by saying, "Cut—Print —Next setup!" And that's it, brothers and sisters, that is your compliment. Not very emotional, is it? But considering the business as a whole, it is a hell of a compliment. That director has your performance on film. You contributed to the film, and a professional bought it. It is a good feeling, and you are going to love it! When you report on the set with the tools this technique puts at your disposal, you will save the director time and involvement that he must concentrate elsewhere. If the director spends little time and says few words to you, do not be alarmed, be pleased. It means that he had confidence in you. When he does speak to you, it will be in relation to the scene, in words that are common between people in the industry, words like *choices, attitudes, wants, needs, little bits of business*. The words describe what a director seeks from the character in a scene.

What has been discussed so far has been Hollywood film productions. By that I mean the weekly television shows that are filmed, and the feature film productions. There are other types of productions in Hollywood that present their own particular problems for the actor. An example of this is "the three camera taped live sitcom shows." How is that for a job? It is hard enough to say, let alone know what to expect after arriving on the set. The live tape shows do give the cast an opportunity to rehearse the show. However, it still presents demands on the actor that are a bit unusual.

Television had a growth pattern that resembled the film industry. Though it has the similarity of film in that it is presented on a screen, that is where the similarity ended as far as the production and technical people were concerned. Television shows were presented on a fixed set. And until videotape was introduced the show was presented from beginning to end. So the production was back to where the stage productions were when films first began to appear. But the intimate appeal that stage has was lost to the audience. The very nature of the television productions that were presented weekly precluded the long rehearsal time for a show that was to be presented once. Techniques were developed for camera, sound, director, and all other production people. The advent of videotape meant only that the show could be viewed at a later date. The techniques that were developed over the years were developed to overcome the lack of the intimate appeal that the stage had, and still have a performance that was patterned after the stage. The impact that film has on the viewer, in that the camera can enlarge or diminish a figure or set a mood, television also had. But film could be shot at different locations. It had mobility for the camera. And above all, it had the time to shoot a scene several ways and then edit the film for the best results. All this had to be done in television, also, but it had to be done differently.

Taped shows, like stage shows, are confined to a fixed set. So each of the disciplines involved in the production has to function within those boundaries. The director must look for the best picture that he can get for the screen from the limited angles that he has. And as with film, economics play a very important part in the production. So each rehearsal is for a specific part of the production. There is a rehearsal for the actor. Then there is a rehearsal for the director, so that he can "block" the show. Then there is a rehearsal for the camera, so that the cameras involved in the show can coordinate their moves with those of the actors. Last, there is a dress rehearsal. Here the combination of all the technical and artistic aspects are run through. These different rehearsals present a new demand on the actor. With each new approach or technique, the actor has to deal from the point of the production people, but also from his own point: remain natural, stay within a character, and hit the marks. With each rehearsal there are changes. The actor must deal with the changes and still give a spontaneous performance. Timing and pacing of the show are very important here, in this type of performance. You will also find yourself doing out-of-context "pickups." These will come after the show has been taped.

These taped shows are performed before a live audience. The producers are seeking spontaneous audience reaction. This presents another demand on the performer. Now you have an audience to play to, but the camera picks up on all of your actions. Which do you play to—the camera or the audience? Actors will debate that for some time to come. I have heard both views expressed and good reasons for each. There is one thing that they all will have to agree on. That is, the camera will pick up on every move and action you make. If you play the part as if you were playing to the person in the last row, the camera will pick it up. It will be enlarged by the camera, and the person watching the show on the screen will see that enlargement. But, on the other hand, the audience is there for the spontaneous reactions, namely laughter! They, too, must see and hear the performance. Once you have mastered the technique that is given in this book, you can make the choice between which one you want to perform to.

Now we enter into another aspect of the film actor's career: commercials. Here the demands are subtle, but in many instances, a trying experience. In commercials you must establish a characterization, add little bits of business, keep the energy level up, sell the product, appear natural, sound sincere, do not sweat, and do it all in a twenty-second time limit—several times! Understand that when these things are told to you they are not meant to frighten you away. Quite the opposite. Though they sound ominous and frightening, they can be accomplished when you have the tools and the knowledge of what to expect. Some commercials will be difficult, but you can succeed through technique.

In the world of television commercials, it has been said that there is more creativity involved than in other Hollywood production. This may or may not be true, but the commercial industry has accomplished what they started out to do, and that is selling products. To sell products, they must get a convincing message directly to the consumer. In the commercial scheme of advertising, the actor stands out. For each creative idea that the advertising men dream up, there must be an actor to bring it to life. For instance, consider what the commercial voice-over actors have done with such products as animated pens, pencils, cats, dogs, etc. They have put personality into these things with the use of their voice and their imagination. Some people in the industry claim that doing voice-over is not really acting. I maintain the opposite. The voice-over person creates a character for the listener or the viewer just as an actor creates one. The only difference is, of course, that the voice-over person is not seen. Radio actors were not seen either. But the fact remains that they had accomplished in radio what television is trying to do today—come directly into the home of the audience and entertain them. There are many classic broadcasts of adventure, mystery, suspense, and romance. The audience was led through the story by the actors and the different sound effects that were developed for radio. These things combined to stir the imagination of the listener. Through the sound of the voice and the phrasing of the dialogue the listener fashioned a physical appearance for himself of the hero or heroine of the story. Radio stimulates the imagination through sound by setting moods with the actor's pacing of his delivery, by his raising or softening of his voice. To me this is acting: convincing the audience that what is happening is truly happening to that actor.

The demands of working in commercials are much the same as they are in any Hollywood production. When you audition for a role you must make choices for a characterization if that is what the script calls for. As a actor this is what you expect. However, this is not always the case. You will find in many instances that what the audition amounts to is some conversation with the producer and director. Or you may be asked to eat some cereal, or drink from a bottle, or perform some other small action.

To understand why these "auditions" for commercials take on so many different forms, let us look back and see what the final purpose is and how to achieve that purpose.

The evolution of the commercial began way back with the

"pitchman" for cure-all medicines. He would travel from town to town in his wagon. At each town he would set up the back of the wagon as a type of stage. Then he would try to attract people to him by having some sort of act performed. The more spectacular the act, the more people would come to watch. The pitchman would sell to the people who came to watch. Obviously, the more people at the wagon, the more potential customers. He soon learned that the better and more spectacular the act, the larger the crowd.

Other businesses of that era tried to take advantage of the ability of entertainment to attract crowds, though they had to be more subtle than the pitchman. They would have print advertising at theaters. Their message was written out on the curtain in the lobbies and other areas in and around the theater.

Advertising agencies developed from these times. It was their job to get the message of the sponsor to as many people as possible. In that message the sponsor's product must be made to look better than any of the competitors. The advertising agencies relied on artwork and magazines. They reached a large number of people through newspapers and magazines. Somehow the advertising agencies never took advantage of motion picture theaters, by presenting commercials on film in the theater. Perhaps it was the lack of sound in the early films. However, when radio began to reach a large number of people, the advertisers saw the potential. Advertising agencies needed a specialized person to deliver the message of the sponsor. These specialists were announcers. But as radio evolved and more and more competition for the attention of the audience arose, a new need arose with it: programs for the listening audience. Again a new medium looked to the actor for the answer. Get the attention of the audience by entertaining them. This was done by the radio actor.

When television began to encroach on the attention of the audience, advertising agencies again stepped in. They had the message of their sponsors delivered as they were delivered over radio—by the specialist, the announcer. But that did not last long. The attention span of the viewer to the announcer on television was so short that it became ineffective. Again, a new industry looked to actors to get the attention of the audience. But this time they wanted the actor to portray a short story about the sponsor's product. A new demand. Over the years this new industry developed a rapport between the actor and the advertising agencies.

The actor in the commercials is always subservient to the product. He is there to make the product look good, or make it look larger or stronger. All the things that the advertiser had for years, through newspaper ads, through radio, he now wanted done visually. His product should not be shown in a bad way, or associated with anything that could reflect badly on it. The competitor's product, on the other hand, could not be shown in a good way if it was within the sponsor's commercial. Essentially, this is the way that the actor should see the demands placed on him in the commercial industry, and the auditions that you will go on will be based from that point of view.

On the actual filming of a commercial, changes are apt to appear quickly and rapidly. For example, you may audition for the role of a mean, gruff truck driver. You make the choices for the role and you win the job. These choices which you have made created a character that you bring with you to the set. When you arrive on the set and are ready to work the director says to you, "By the way, do you have the new lines?" "No," you reply. "Oh well, here they are. We had to change them and, by the way, please soften the character because we don't want people to think that bad characters come to our locations."

This situation actually happened to me; it was an extreme one. Imagine if it happened to an actor who had just arrived in Hollywood. If an inexperienced actor were confronted with those demands, he might go into a temper tantrum, and justifiably so, but he would lose in the long run—or he could take some time away from the camera, study the new lines, and work out a new character. If he chose the first way of handling the situation, the director would be a little disturbed, even though he is aware that the sponsor made an unreasonable demand. The display of temper over the situation could set off a chain reaction that could stifle or even end a potentially successful Hollywood career. If the actor was prepared for changes and took the second approach, he could work something out and wing it. You cannot give a top-level performance with excellent choices at a moment's notice. The director knows that. He is aware of the actor's problems, but he expects the actor to give him something. He must have something to work with. Directors, producers, and all the other people involved in production want you to do a good job. They will bend over backward to help you to that end.

In Hollywood, the trial-and-error method on the set is not tolerated. You are expected to have an understanding of the many and varied demands that film has. If you cannot at a given time bring out the requirements of a scene, the director may cut the scene. Or if it is a pickup within a scene, he may drop that if he feels that you are not coming up to the standards. So when you report on the set to work, it is necessary that you have at your fingertips the many different emotions that you may have to display. You may not need them on one job, but sometimes or another you will be required to display many of them.

Film requires a natural delivery from you, natural in both dialogue and physical actions. The lens can and does magnify your actions, and, consequently, you will find that you must reduce the delivery of your movements as the camera gets closer. You must understand how far you can take a particular movement when that movement was done once in a scene and must be repeated with a different camera angle or distance. You must understand the intensity of an emotion from the camera's point of view. You must understand them so that you can repeat them in different degrees when you are required to do so, and still make them appear natural. You will have to become familiar with the physical reactions that are common to people so that it is understood by the viewer what you are feeling and in what degree. Again, it must be so familiar to you that you can do it naturally. When a scene requires that you react to a situation without dialogue and without other actors, you must have at your command the physical manifestations needed to bring the point of the scene to the viewer.

The previous descriptions are intended to illustrate why this technique was written into this book. Acting is an art, but filmmaking goes one step further: it combines many disciplines that are directed toward one goal—the performance of the actor. The actor must be prepared to work with these disciplines. When he is, the final work can be a work of art.

Hollywood Film Acting

Part I

THE CRAFT

Economic Levels: The Beginning in Breaking Down a Characterization

Actors in the film industry are very often required to make quick decisions for different characterizations. And usually these decisions must be made with the minimum amount of information. Characterization changes may occur on the set while you are shooting. This is one of the demands that the film industry expects you to be aware of. Further, they expect that you will be able to perform a character change as required. You, as the actor, will face auditions that have the same demands. They will ask for a reading in one or more different ways. Many times your creativity in the characterizing at an audition will win the job for you, because at the auditions they are looking for something different. And when they are looking for something different they usually mean a different kind of character. At an audition you are given the very basics about the role that you are trying for. From this small amount of information you must build something for the people you are auditioning for, to see and to determine from this that you can do a better job than the other actors trying for the same part. When you do win the job, you must come to the set with a character already constructed. And this is to be done without the benefit of other actors to work with—a real challenge, I realize that, but not impossible. The way that you would do it is through your own imagination and talent. But to utilize your talent you should have the tools that can display your choices. When you begin to use the tools, it begins to become easier and easier to display your talent.

Each actor who has performed or will perform or even audition will experience nerves. This nervousness is natural. What you must do is to direct it. In breaking down a character, and in performing that character, you are to utilize the nervousness that you experience. You are to do that through the different choices you will make. These choices will be made through the different exercises that you can practice from this technique. The first of these is the "Economic Level."

Your energy is often internal, and you must find the key to bring it to the surface. On the stage you can bring the energy out to work for you through the benefit of rehearsal. When you rehearse you change the "unknown," to the "known." You know what you are going to use in your characterization, you know what the other actors are going to do, and you know how you are to respond to them. In film these things are not known until you reach the set and start shooting. The source of "nerves," then, we can safely say, is the "unknown", that is to say, we do not know what is in store for us. Consequently, we are not certain of how we are to respond. If you know how you are going to respond, then the "nerves" will correspondingly be reduced. They will be reduced, and those nerves which you still have will be put to use. In film you will direct that energy throughout your body and into productive actions.

Before you begin your practice sessions you may find your body stiff and unresponsive. The building up of nervous energy can have this effect on you, especially before an actual performance. Many actors have their own particular way of releasing suppressed energy. Here we are going to concentrate on one specific method of releasing suppressed energy that is designed to both release energy and to heighten energy. You should begin with the following steps: (1) stand erect, (2) breathe deeply, and (3) extend your arms in front of you parallel to the floor. Your next motion is to move your arm alongside of you, behind you, then back to the front again. Extend your fingers to the extreme and breathe deeply while making the arm motions. A low energy can be traced to low oxygen content in the bloodstream, and a case of nerves will burn the oxygen very fast. When you breathe deeply you are simply replacing the oxygen that your nerves have exhausted. By stretching your arms and legs you can help to increase the flow of blood through your body. This stretching is similar to isometrics. It has the same effect that isometrics have on your body: you "feel" better. Your body becomes loose, your movements are smoother. This loosening effect will also smoothen out the voice quality. Your voice can display nervousness also. If, after the exercises, your voice is still uneven, you can correct that rather simply: shout—during the exercises. Bring your voice to its maximum while you are stretching and push the air out till your lungs are empty. After a few times at these exercises you will see the calming effect it has on you. You may find that these exercises work better for you if you add some different manners and applications to them. That is good; whatever works best for you is what you apply. These are suggestions that you will work from; they are not the end all for everyone.

The loosening up exercises are to be performed before each practice session. You should get used to doing them so that when you are at an audition or on the set you are familiar with the manner that best loosens you up. That is when they are to be applied. The purpose is to have you in control when it counts. Before you go into an audition you should loosen up. It is not necessary to perform the exercises at the audition; rather, you may do them before you leave the home. Then you continue with the breathing exercises.

The exercises will direct the nervousness to energy. Now we begin to direct that energy. You will take the energy and put it into "energy releases." The energy releases are what you are to use to display your character for the scene. These are the choices that you will make for the character you are to play. Again, there are no rehearsals that you can use to search for different ways to accomplish the final result. So to begin to break your character down, we are going to divide people into class levels, or economic levels. That is to say that one particular character could be portrayed in different ways—three different ways to be specific. A character could be one of three different classes: high class, middle class, or low class. Each class has its own particular manner about it. The different manner in which the class is displayed will be the energy releases that you will utilize. Operating from one of these three economic levels, you will direct the energy to outward manifestations of the character's economic level. You will make individual choices for energy releases that will go from manner of walking and talking to use of hands, eyes, or feet. The more that you perform the practice sessions within an economic level, the more adept you will become at getting into character. Then you will not need rehearsal for your characterization.

We have now broken the character down to one of three classes. So we must know what are the physical manifestations particular to each of the three classes. The energy releases must be visual. All of the choices for energy releases are to be physical. So we look for the release in that area.

Let us begin with the low class. Usually you will find that poor posture is inherent at this class level and you will assume the posture of the character. Perhaps the shoulders are sloped down so that the arms are hanging loosely at the side. The stomach is pushed forward and the muscles are relaxed. The head is thrust forward a little to compensate for the sloping shoulders. Now you are to walk in this posture. In walking this character uses his feet as indifferently as he uses the rest of his body. His feet fall to the floor so that they make a sound as they land. You can practice this by walking around the room in this posture. Remember that the shoulders, the head, the stomach, and the feet must be in coordination with each other; they must all display the economic level you are portraying.

By walking around the room you will begin to find releases for your nervousness. For example you could give your character some habits. Let us look at how you can release energy habits and make it appear that it is a habit of the character. As you are walking around the room you can twitch one of your hands or you can put your hands in your pockets or take out a handkerchief. You make other choices; these are to show you what the personal habits of a character can be. It is movements such as these which would allow you to release energy through your hands.

Let us go into the second economic level, the middle class. We again begin with posture. Remember that these choices are twofold in usage: firstly to be visual for the camera and secondly to release energy. In the middle class you would stand more erect. Your spine is much straighter and your head is held up. Your arms would be held at the side and your walk would be firm. The walk and posture are distinctly middle class. What we might say is that the middle class person seems to resist gravity where the low class person seems to give in to gravity. Again you practice this by walking around the room in this posture. While walking in circles or figure eights stop to look around for a moment then continue to move in the posture of the middle-class person. Bring the energy up through the spine using your body to release nervous energy. To add more releases choose some habits for your character. Use your imagination. Put yourself up for comparison. See what you would do as far as habits are concerned. Borrow from the people that you know use some of their habits. Choose movements of the hands and feet the eyes or a combination of all three. While you are walking change the mood of the character. Later in the book we will get into the specific moods and how they are displayed. For now you should begin by thinking of energy releases that are familiar to you.

Finally we will discuss the third economic level, the upper class. You will begin again with the posture. You as the character would stand more erect. Your shoulders would be straight as well as the spine. Your head should be held straight so that the chin is jutting out slightly. Your mouth would probably be closed with the lips slightly puckered. Your arms would show complete control emanating complete confidence. The walk is distinctive. All your motions should be a calculated move to create an effect or image. You will walk around the room in this posture stop assume other postures and make some choices and actions for your character (i.e. eyes, lips, legs, hands, etc.). For this class make your character appear to rise above gravity. Make the motion efficiently. When nervousness appears make some choices for energy releases. Make those choices something that you are familiar with.

In performing the exercises for energy releases you should be very broad and unrestricted: you should be larger than life. The movements will at first appear unnatural and artificial but you can always tone that down. Eventually you will be able to run through these exercises in different degrees. When you achieve a few roles in film the degree to which you display these energy releases will be a decision you will have to make. Therefore, if you know how to be unrestricted in your choices you will be able to choose from a variety of areas that best fit the role of the character. For example, if a character from the upper class is to become hysterical, then the actor would have to be quite broad in his choices. If the director thinks that the choices are too broad for the scene then he will bring the level down. From a directorial point of view it is much easier to bring an actor down, than it is to bring him up.

As you progress through the energy releases you will develop some that are particularly helpful to you yet do not seem to work for others. However, you should not shut your mind to the suggestions and techniques of other actors because they may have an answer to some problem that you at one time or another may have with characterization. Sometimes you may become discouraged when a case of nerves becomes obvious and energy releases do not seem to help. I know an actor who had this problem on one particular show: his hands shook. The actor was playing the part of a junkie on a popular network detective series. The night before his filming he worked his nervous hands into a habit of the character. He also added an occasional wetting of the lips as well as the darting of his eyes from side to side to the characterization. All these characteristics were brought together by the actor in order to establish his role as one of a nervous junkie. It all worked so well that he was congratulated by the director and the star of the show. What that actor did was to direct his energy. Instead of trying to suppress that energy he redirected it into a habit of the character. He did this without the benefit of other actors or rehearsals. He drew upon his knowledge of characterizations and he creatively applied it.

The habits that you create for your character roles will serve you well through the "one-liners" and "bit parts" that you will obtain in films. These parts are not all that simple to perform. On the contrary, you will not have much time to develop a character. However, if you utilize the three economic levels in your preparation you will certainly be ahead in your character development, even if it is only one line! You should practice the three levels so that you appear natural, and almost graceful. And you should not be sporatic. Focus on your manifestations, and do not allow them to dissipate. The commercial roles that you will win, and the auditions that you are presented with, are as demanding as the bit parts. Therefore, you should apply the same technique when you prepare for a commercial job. If your part runs from ten seconds to ten pages, the breakdown of the character, in regard to the economic level, is the same.

There is another area that you are concerned with, in which the economic level is applied, and it comes under the heading of auditions. Here, you must think on your feet, and the breakdown of the economic levels can help you to narrow the area of your choices. Actually, the area of auditions is in a separate category, and I do not want to discuss it now. However, you will have a definite advantage over other actors who do not break their characters down from that point. With all the advantages for using the economic levels, I hope that you see the value of practicing them. Also, if you feel that your energy is slipping, go into breathing exercises.

The energy can be measured for our purposes in two degrees: good or bad. If it is good, then the choices are working for the actor and the audience will watch. If the energy level is not correct, then the audience will stop watching that actor and look at another actor or another show! So get familiar with those economic levels. The audience is the final judge. If they believe you, then you have done your job as an actor. They will believe you if you perform naturally. You can perform naturally if you are familiar with the choices that you have made.

2

The Physical Senses

When an actor is in character, he portrays that character both vocally and physically. The writer has certain ideas in his script that convey thoughts through speech, but this is only one of the senses. The writer wants the audience to know what the character feels or thinks in a particular situation even if there are no lines. To approach this problem, the film actor has to work toward a solution without the benefit of other actors. This is what you must do. The actor's responses to a given set of circumstances within a scene are shot in a "master" and then shot as "pickups." A master is a series of wide-angled shots used in filming a total sequence of actions within a scene. *Pickup* is a term used to describe added close-up shots of actors within that scene. In shooting close-ups of a single actor, the director may place another actor off-camera to give the on-camera actor someone with whom he can react. However, only the on-camera actor appears on the screen. In the next series of shots the actors may be reversed and the other actor then does his close-ups. The finished scene in this example will show both actors interacting with each other on the screen. Naturally, if there is no dialogue in the scene, then the reactions of the on-camera actor are strictly physical reactions to the circumstances of the scene. The camera sees only the actor in the lens; therefore, the audience shares the same view. On stage, the actor must be correct in the physical reaction neeed, but the distance between him and the audience works for his benefit. The audience has full view of all the activities on the stage, including other actors, stage setting, props, etc. The stage actor will depend on his entire body to express character portrayal, and, because of the distance from the audience, he must magnify his action tenfold. In film, the actor must be just as accurate in using his physical senses, but since he is viewed through a camera lens, his actions must be localized (i.e., centered around the face, the eyes, a single hand, etc.). The film actor must have control of his physical senses on a wider range. He must be able to go from very broad to very narrow and still be convincing within the response.

Our senses are the different ways that nature has provided for our survival. They send to the brain messages of danger, of pleasure, or of pain. Through the senses we display emotion; we kiss to show love, we touch to show love or the feeling for another person or object. A sudden start, danger, and surprise are the manifestations of all five of the senses, and until we are certain we are in no danger all, five senses are focused toward the source until the facts are evaluated. You as an actor must be aware of this. You must use your senses with conscious control, because though a scene may have danger in it for the character you are portraying, you as the actor know there is no danger for you personally.

You must have the knowledge and the control of the five senses to be able to demonstrate to the audience what you are feeling or thinking, and be able to display any one or all of them on demand. Further, you must do it gracefully and even poetically.

I am certain that you know what the five senses are and how they function. However, I am going to repeat them for you, so as to avoid doubt in the coming exercises. Also, you must be aware of the senses, as tools in the film business. Practice and repetition will make the senses appear natural and real, when you are called upon to use them out of context, and when there is no other actor to relate to, or "play off of." Since we tend to take matters rather lightly, when we are called upon to display some feeling or emotion that we have experienced, we have to search our memories for an answer. If we can respond through past experience, then we can utilize it in presenting a characterization. However, because when we reacted to some situation we did it instinctively, we must study our own actions. Like anything that is studied, the performing of an emotion or feeling could appear unnatural or "studied." This is especially true if the performance had originally been played with another actor and if the present situation demands that you play alone to the camera.

Now, you will practice all the senses in different situations. Each one of those senses will be one that you have displayed before; they will all be familiar to you. Your awareness of the physical manifestations of those senses will give you such complete control that, if a director wants you to tone it down, you will be able to do it without losing the energy or the emotion. Now, if you were a director, how would you feel about an actor who could do that for you?

The following are the five senses that you will be dealing with: (1) sight, (2) hearing, (3) smell, (4) taste, (5) touch.

Sight

For this sense you obviously use your eyes. Sometimes you see clearly, yet other times you must strain to see; you must focus. Vision stimulates collected memories, opinions. Eyes are the windows to the soul. They show anger, fear, etc.

Hearing

You use this sense in a multiawareness capacity. Through your ears, you are capable of classifying sounds simultaneously. Think about the different sounds you hear in an ordinary situation, and note your reactions to them within your own mind. Remember that, unlike sight, hearing is a 360-degree sense. For instance, you will hear other actors saying their lines in a scene even though they are behind you. Therefore you must bring awareness to this scene through hearing. As an exercise, note in your mind your reactions to the following: simple noises; loud, shrill noises; then soft, pleasant music.

Smell

This is the strongest sense through memory. Smelling is done in two ways: (1) through the nostrils to the olfactory nerves, and (2) through the mouth by pushing air over food, then directly to the olfactory nerves and, finally, to the brain. When you have a cold there is a coating on the tongue that diminishes the sense of smell. Smells are said to be moist vapors and, since sight and smell are closely related, you should think of scents as colored vapors (i.e., the smell of rich, brown coffee). We can classify the types of odors as: (1) fragrant, flowery, saccharine; (2) acid, sour; (3) burnt, pugent, musk; (4) repulsive, putrid. Smells, pleasant or unpleasant, you can recall by association. When the need arises, say to yourself, "it smells like," and your mind will fill in the answer.

Taste

The sense of taste varies with age. Our taste buds lose some of their sensitivity as we get older. Our saliva is as individual as our fingerprints: it is our acid neutralizer. The tongue has areas that deal with individual classifications of taste. The types of taste are: (1) sweet—tip of the tongue; (2) sour—sides of the tongue; (3) salty—tip and all around the sides; (4) bitter—back of the tongue and upper surface. (Note: During the day you should become aware when you first begin to taste liquids.)

Touch

This sense is defined as electrical vibrations experienced by the receiver we live in, our skin. We can literally see through the millions of nerve "eyes" all over us. Our skin is our expandable antenna of awareness, just as a cat's whiskers are its antennae. Our touch transmits signals to the brain, through texture and temperature sensations. Touching is the process of sending or receiving heat. Every texture of skin has a temperature. The eyes, on the other hand, are insensitive to heat or cold.

In using the senses for scene work, you must first become aware of your reactions to stimulants in all the senses, individually and collectively. How would you react to a liquid that you have tasted before, and now tastes slightly different? How broad would your reactions be if the difference were great? How do you react to stimulants of the senses of smell? These are the things that you must observe about yourself, and then rehearse, so that when those stimulants are not present but you must act as though they are, you can convince an audience that they actually are there and affecting you. You should observe the reactions of people around you and their responses to stimulants. Then compare their reactions to yours. Your reactions to stimulants in a scene that you are performing in must be understood by the viewer as to cause and effect. When a person is cold, his entire body reacts to the cold. When you are in this situation you shiver, rub your arms, and move your legs up and down. Do you know why you do these things? These body movements bring the blood to the surface of your skin, and circulate the blood through the body at a faster rate. When you walk into a room that is warm, what do you do? You remove your outer clothing and begin to warm yourself. The most sensitive are the hands. Most probably you would rub them to stimulate circulation there. If this scene were being filmed, the camera would have picked you up as you walked into the room. What choices would you use to show that you are cold? You could still be rubbing your hands or cupping your ears. By concentrating on the parts of the body that are the most sensitive to cold you can demonstrate that you are. So remember that the sense reaction to cold is touch.

Let us take another scene. Here the conditions are the same as the previous scene. The sun is blazing, the temperature is hot—and you are very thirsty. You have come upon a water hole. But the water does not look very fresh. However, you have to taste the water to find out. Now this may seem rather obvious, but you must remember to utilize all the senses here, and not just the sense of thirst. You would be surprised at the number of actors who would do a great job with the sense of thirst (tasting the water, spitting it out), but would forget to utilize the senses of sight and touch, necessary to illustrate the sun, heat, etc. I have watched scenes in which something was misleading, but I could not focus on the problem area. I am sure that you can recall a similar experience. Somewhere in a scene, believability can fall away to confusion, if the senses are improperly used and if they do not follow in logical sequence. As an example, I am going to use the scene already described. It is a hot day, the sun is blazing, the actor is thirsty, and there is only putrid water to drink. He walks into the scene utilizing the sense of sight and the sense of taste, but he neglects the sense of touch. Therefore, we now have a thirsty character standing in the blazzing sun who does not look hot. Without the sense of touch to establish that the character is hot, the scene loses believability. Imagine that you are the director who shot that scene. With all the elements involved in being the director, you may have overlooked the fact that something was indeed missing in the performance. When you look at the "rushes" the next day, you see the problem. Now you have two choices: (1) shoot the entire scene over again with the added expenses involved, or (2) use it, regardless of the mistakes.

Each choice has its drawbacks. If you shoot the scene over, it will mean extra time and money. If you use the scene as it is, it could diminish the quality of the entire production. As the director, would you remember that actor favorably?

We will now attempt a scene where the demands are a little different. The character you are playing is an alcoholic who has not had a drink in several days. At one time the character was quite successful. He had a family, and he was very devoted to them. He was deeply in love with his wife, who had run away with another man. So, in turn, he turned to alcohol. The scene takes place in New York's Bowery. There are no lines in the scene. The Bowery, with its many restaurants and bars, is busy with people. There are sounds of a festive attitude heard through the open doors. As the character passes a bar, he hears his wife's favorite song being played on a piano. It is a pleasant summer evening. Our character is crippled by remorse and self-pity.

The problems in this scene are obvious, and by utilizing the sense reactions and breaking down the character into class we can make some valid choices. First of all, let us look at the class. Since he is an alcoholic and on the Bowery, we can place him into a lower class. Thirdly, we add the habits of an alcoholic. Tuning the senses to touch, we must remember that he has not had a drink in several days. Now, how would he utilize the senses? It does not matter where our character is going, and his feet can illustrate this in his walk. The piano playing could key the sense of hearing in the character to the past and his wife. The character could take a worn photo from his pocket when the sense of hearing is keyed. Think of as many ways as possible to use all of the senses, then emphasize one of them while utilizing the others.

There is no real solution to the problem that I have just set up for you. It is simply an exercise. But, in place of a solution, you can make the scene interesting or you can make the scene dull; right and wrong are not valid here. In selecting your choices, choose the sensory reaction that works most interestingly for you. However, do not neglect the others, but use them to support your prime selection. If you find that the energy level is dropping on the sense of sight, then switch to the sense of smell, and so on, until you find the one that is most natural and works best for the scene. All of your senses are interrelated, and if, while you are doing a scene, you have trouble with one of the senses, let another sense help you. Allow each and every sense to work for you, so that you attain a complete awareness as the character in that scene.

We have previously covered the senses of touch, taste, sight, and hearing. We shall now discuss the sense of smell. Instead of using one exercise scene to illustrate this sense, we shall include it in a series of exercises.

In these scenes you shall perform without dialogue, yet you will convey to the audience exactly what you are doing and feeling. The scene is set up with a set of instructions. These signify the demands that you will face with real scripts; treat them with that respect. These instructions will tell you the following: time of day, temperature, and what you are doing in relation to your surroundings, i.e., your action. You are to utilize all five senses in one way or another. You are not to use any dialogue or sounds. If the temperature is comfortable, then be comfortable. If the temperature is an uncomfortable one, then show that too.

Exercise Scene 1

You are walking down a railroad track into the country. It is a nice sunny day. The birds are singing and it is spring and the temperature is warm. You have not eaten since breakfast; it is now noon.

Exercise Scene 2

You enter a friendly tavern in ski country. It is cold outside and it is snowing. You come to this tavern once a week for friendly conversation and a drink. You always walk from your cabin to this tavern. You are dressed in heavy, warm clothes. After a while you get very warm, and you try to open a window. The window is stuck, and you cannot open it. One of your companions walks to the window and, with very little effort, opens it.

Exercise Scene 3

You are an office worker. The time is seven in the morning. You are in your own room, and the room is cold. You are late for work. You are a heavy smoker and cannot find your cigarettes. After a search you find the cigarettes, and you leave for work.

Exercise Scene 4

It is twelve o'clock noon on Sunday. You were out all night drinking. You did not get home until dawn. Your clothes are strewn about the room. You are a heavy smoker. The window shades were left up, and you have just awakened. The temperature is comfortable.

Exercise Scene 5

In this scene I want you to utilize all five senses. You are out for an evening stroll. The scene is a small city. You are on a street that has all kinds of shops. Many people are walking, and there are festive sounds all about. It is a hot summer evening.

Exercise Scene 6

It is late in the evening. You have just arrived home. You open the front door and feel for the light switch. Nothing happens when you flick the switch. A bulb has burned out and you must replace it.

Exercise Scene 7

You are in the hospital recovering from an eye operation. You are sitting in a chair, and you ring for the nurse to bring you a glass of water. She does not arrive as quickly as you would like, so you get your own water. The nurse arrives as you are drinking the water.

Exercise Scene 8

You are sitting at home in your favorite chair, reading a book, and a fire has started. At first you do not see or hear anything unusual. All of a sudden the fire bursts into the room.

Exercise Scene 9

You are in a bar. You have just received a drink from a person that you suspect wants to kill you. The bar is hot and smoky.

These exercises have covered all five senses. There is a prime sensory reaction in each one of the scenes, but all senses should be fully utilized. You should get to the point of the scene in logical sequence. You can take your time utilizing each sense, but do not extend it to the point of boredom. Do not be afraid to experiment, because this is the time and place to try out new approaches. Focus your energy on the objective of the scene, and release your energy through the sensory choices. For example, when you are trying to open the window in Exercise Scene 2, that window is your only objective. Your energy is focused on the window, and it is released through your sensory choices.

After you have performed these exercises several times, and have gotten a feel for the scene, begin to apply the class of the characters, i.e., lower, middle, or upper class. For these exercises you may apply any class you wish to the character of the scene. The exercises are to be performed broad and unrestricted. If you have someone to view your performance, do not be concerned with perfection; do not "push for results." Invariably, they will give you a critical dissertation on the inner feelings of the character, and how the scene should have been performed. Instead of seeking such a critique, ask them if you appeared cold, hot, or thirsty. Also, ask your viewers what class you appeared to be representing. Whoever is watching should understand what sensory reaction the character experienced in the scene.

When you apply the class structure to the characters in the different scenes, you may find that the class choice does not always come across as it should. Do not panic! Society is made up of all kinds of people in all three class structures. Think about the many varying facets that illustrate class distinction. I have given you suggestions for each class. But you may arrive at a different approach that is much more workable for you. For the present, keep the following formula in mind: lower class gives in to gravity; middle class resists gravity; and upper class rises above gravity. In your exercises, apply the tools as you see them. The terms *good* and *bad* do not apply to acting. The only terms that apply are *interesting* and *boring*.

3

Moods and Emotions

I have discussed the outward manifestations of the character in relation to outside influences, and you should now be in a position to practice sensory reactions to the five senses: sight, sound, taste, touch, and hearing. At this point, you should be able to break a character down to a level of understanding and, without rehearsal, demonstrate to an audience the class of the character and his reaction to his immediate circumstance, that is, what pleases him and what does not. When you get a script now, the fear of the unknown should be diminished somewhat, because you have developed some of the tools necessary to an understanding of the Hollywood scene. Confidence will begin to appear, because now you can do some "homework" on your characterization. Now, you can focus your talents to the needs and demands of the scene. If the scene calls for you to be cold, you can act cold, even though the temperature under the lights reaches one hundred degrees! If the directions you receive are last-minute changes—and they are the opposite of what you expected—you can use your awareness and technique in dealing with them.

We must now deal with character emotions and how they must be used on the set. In working with a scene, the director will speak of emotions of the character in the same way in which he spoke of reactions. For example, he will say, "You are cold and hungry. Action!" You will be able to deal with that direction. However, if he says, "You are cold and hungry, and angry. Then you see food and shelter, and you become happy. Action!" Then he has told you to change your mood from being angry to being happy, within the sensory reactions. You have sensory reactions fairly well in mind now, but could you solve the problem of mood changes in this situation? That question will be answered in the following discussion.

To bring moods into the realm of technique we must be consciously aware of them, as we have come to be with the senses. You know what moods are, in fact you are probably quite good at displaying your moods! But, how about displaying the mood of a character in a scene? In most cases, the mood of the character is just the opposite of the mood that you happen to be in at the time. When the time comes, will you be able to display a certain mood? Also, suppose the mood of the character is to change once or even twice during a scene. Could you do this? Suppose you "feel" the mood do not make it clear to the audience. We have all seen actors like that! These actors feel the scene, but their physical movements remain the same throughout. They are called "one-level actors," because their feelings remain inside where no one can see them. They are very intense and very deep, but their physical appearance is always the same. Their outward appearances are likely to be the same when they are making love as when they are in grave danger: their anger is the same as their joy. Their savior is the versatile actor who is in the scene with them. It is this other actor, or group of actors as the case may be, who makes the scene come to life. In most cases, a versatile actor has to work twice as hard to maintain scene believability when he is playing opposite a one-level actor. Personally, I prefer interesting actors, and so does Hollywood!

To bring the moods to your conscious mind, we must break them down into specifics. We start by labeling the moods that people have, and, from this point, we will call for labels when we are seeking moods. You should practice these labels in the same way in which you practiced the senses. First, the labels will be practiced by themselves. You will be given labels to perform, without any additional demands. The labels are designed to convince the audience that you really feel the mood of the character. If the audience believes you, then you have done your job. Since moods sometimes present problems for actors, it might be better to add character demands, or utilizing of the senses. Many people resent showing their feelings, and you may need the added support of the senses. With that, we will begin to work on these labels.

To begin our subject on labels, you must start by being broad and unrestricted in your performance. After you have utilized the labels in a broad sense, you must tone everything down. The practice sessions are to be performed while you are sitting in a chair. You are not permitted to use props of any kind. Instead, use your body to express the emotions. Dialogue will be used in the practice sessions; it is included for timing. Also, you may use the dialogue to demonstrate the labels.

Mood Labeling

Joy

Joy is the emotion evoked by well-being, success, or the hope of possessing what one desires. Joy is expressing delight or pleasure. This mood is expressed through your face. Joy is expressed by resisting gravity, as in the middle class discussed in the previous chapter. Physically speaking, it takes fewer muscles to express joy than to express sadness. First of all, the facial muscles lift up, so that the eyes smile. From this point, the muscles lift higher up to show a grin, and higher still to show a smile.

Anger

Anger is a general term for describing a strong feeling of displeasure. Physically, anger is expressed through a flaring of the eyes, tightening of the lips, and an overall tensing of the body.

Sadness

Sadness is the emotion evoked by the lack of well-being; it is the opposite of joy. Sadness is easily detectable in the facial area: the eyes are cast down; the muscles around the eyes, cheeks, and mouth are drawn downward.

Laughter

Laughter is an expression of joy. It is an expression that uses all of the physical features of joy, with the added feature of sound.

Tearing

Tearing is the act of weeping or grieving. This expression can denote joy or sadness. The crying of tears is a physical release.

Fear

Fear is an unpleasant, often strong emotion of anticipation or awareness of danger.

These are the labels we will use in our practice sessions. They are meant to identify the mood of the character, according to the demands of the scene. Each of the labels has degrees that you can demonstrate to the audience. Each mood is not a steadfast and rigid expression. The labels are not rituals that you perform, but instead are to be used as a vehicle to get the idea of the scene to the audience. Anger, for example, is different when you direct it to a child than when you direct it to an adult. Even when you direct it to an adult, it has varying degrees. You can be "mad" at a friend, because of something they said. Again, you can be angered when someone invades your home. We have fears of getting a traffic ticket from a policeman, but there are fears that we have of the night, and of injury too. So you see, these labels are the basis from which you live and operate. You are an individual, therefore your manner of expression for these labels should have your own personal imprint on them. However, they should be understood by the audience. Do not develop a set manner for expressing one label and let it go at that. It would be just as boring as being a one-level actor. Your performance would be predictable throughout each film that you did.

The intensity of a mood shows through the eyes, therefore you must learn to control that intensity from within as well as without. Onstage the intensity in the eyes is not as obvious as it is when you have a close-up on film. Therefore you will have to learn to cut the intensity in half for the close-up; you will learn this technique through practice. You cannot keep a mood within you and not show it to an audience, otherwise you will become a boring or one-level actor. You will now begin to rehearse the balance between the two extremes. You will not rehearse with another actor in these practice sessions. You will rehearse alone onstage, or wherever you choose to work. You will be given the labels, and you will be told to demonstrate them.

To help you in getting into the labels, remember to focus on that label. Do not scatter your energy all over the place, but zero in on the label, bringing your senses along with that targeting. Bring the intensity to the eyes, and be broad and unrestricted in the beginning; in the beginning be broad in acting out all these labels. First of all, you have to find your limit before you can begin to tone it down. Next, you will begin to subtract degrees from the various labels. But, again, in the beginning you must be broad. You are going to be required to be broad without the use of your hands and feet. This may be difficult, but it will be rewarding. Remember, take your time getting to the labels.

Now, I told you earlier in this chapter that you would be using dialogue in these exercises for timing. That is correct. However, we are concerned with the timing of the transition from one label to another, and not for length of performance. As with the practice scenes in sensory reaction, do not overdo it to the point where it will become boring. This timing may take a while to acquire, and do not worry if it does not work smoothly for you now, but do not overlook it either. Work your way into the opening label-take the time— when you think you have it, begin your dialogue. After you practice these exercises, you will be able to shorten the time required to get into the opening label.

When your label is tears, then shed tears. Use whatever way you have to, to bring tears out. Other than that I have no suggestions to offer as to method to get the tears to flow. I know some actors who can bring tears to their eyes at a moment's notice. Yet others, like myself, cannot bring them out at all. However, I can convince the audience that I am crying and, for the close-ups on film, I have used glycerol. Even when you use props, such as the glycerol, you must be able to show emotion. So, if you find objections to the value of labels, answer this question. How would you feel about an actor in a close-up with tears streaming down his face and no emotion being expressed in any other way? It would not work, right? Of course not! It would be like the one-level actor, or the missing sensory reaction. You would have all the elements for the label, but what it takes to weld those elements together is missing. What does it take to weld those elements? It takes an actor who knows what the different sensory reactions are, and the manner in which they work together. Technique! If all of this were not so, then the film industry could use anyone off the street to perform. When you have the technique at your command, you can convince the audience that you feel a certain way, even though you do not actually feel that way.

A few directions about the practice sessions are in order, at this point. First of all, we are using nursery rhymes! That is right! You will sit in a chair and recite nursery rhymes, like "Humpty Dumpty" and "Mary Had a Little Lamb."

Interesting, huh? Grown people reciting these things. Well do not despair; it is for a very good reason. You see, when you recite these things, you must bring out all the emotion you can. I have found that if you can bring emotion to something completely meaningless to you, it will help when you are working a film or commercial in which you cannot completely grasp the meaning of the lines, because you are not affected by those lines.

The result of this thinking has been these exercises. You will say these exercises with different labels at the opening and at the closing. But the labels must be visual. I said before that you can use the voice to illustrate a label, but not the voice alone. When you do voice-over work, you will find that it sometimes helps to act out the lines you are saying. For those of you out there who have those golden pipes, and can express emotion through the voice alone, forget it! You must act out the label.

Now to begin, first I will present to you, the lines. These are your lines for Scene 1M:

> Mary had a little lamb.
> Its fleece was white as snow.
> Everywhere that Mary went
> The lamb was sure to go.

Now for the lines in scene 2M:

> Humpty Dumpty sat on a wall.
> Humpty Dumpty had a great fall.
> All the King's horses
> And all the King's men
> Couldn't put Humpty Dumpty
> Together again.

I sincerely hope that many of you out there think that this will be simple, because if you do think that, then you will find that surprises are in store for you. If you do happen to find that the exercises are easy for you, that is good, but practice anyway. Sometimes you will think that the exercises are easy, but nobody in the audience knows one label from another. That is not good! After all, your job as an actor is to convince the audience, and do it with ease. If one of the two of the above is missing, then it might be wise to either practice or find another profession.

For the first exercise, we will use Scene 1M. Remember to take your time getting to that first label, and build up to it. If this were a workshop they would say, "Action," and you would begin your scene, continuing until you heard them say, "Cut." You would remain in your closing label until then, even if your lines were completed. To compensate for the lack of an instructor, you are to vary the timing in your scene. This is to include the time it takes to speak your lines, as well as the time you are to remain in your closing label. In building up to your closing label, begin that buildup as soon as you can.

Now for your first try, using scene 1M.

> Your opening label is: joy.
> Your closing label is: anger.

Take your time getting to that opening label. Say the lines slowly and take your time. Do not hurry the lines. And do not begin your opening line until you think you have a grasp on that opening label. Try it once, then go back and try it again. When you go back, I want you to consciously think about where that transition from one label to the next will occur within that scene. You have four lines, say them, get a feel of the time it takes to get through them; it isn't very long. Now try it again, and remember—the emotion is joy. When you have it down, begin. The joy must drop, and give way to anger. The anger can be built up to, or it can be an abrupt change. If it is built up to, then the transition should be slow and thoughtful. If it is abrupt, then it can be done on a line, or even a word. Vary it, by speaking the lines quickly with the corresponding label changes. Do not move from that chair! Do not move your hands! Let your body respond to the label. Let the anger and joy show through your eyes and your entire body.

Let us continue. Using Scene 1M, go through the labels, beginning with joy as your opening label. The next exercise would be with a closing label of sadness. Next, your opening label is anger. Go through the labels until you have some control over them, regardless of where they appear in the scene. With each exercise you are to vary the time it takes you to speak the lines. With each exercise you are to vary the mood transitions from gradual to abrupt.

Now we will begin on Scene 2M. Here, everything applies, as it did in Scene 1M. However, we have one more transition to perform. That is to say, you now have to use three labels. All you have, by way of additional dialogue is two more lines. Of course you are not in a hurry, are you? The variation in a line delivery is to be from slow, to moderate, to quick. The pauses are to be varied, as the lines are varied, and the transitions are to be varied, too.

To start you off on this three-label scene, I suggest that your opening label be joy and your closing label, anger, with an additional label of sadness. If you find yourself fumbling in a scene, do not worry about it. It is better that you fumble here than when you are on the set. Also, your fumbling will decrease in direct relation to the number of times you practice your labels.

If you are applying this technique by yourself, then I suggest you get a friend to call the scenes for you, after you have practiced them with their variations. All he or she has to do is call "Action" and "Cut." Also, he should tell you if you appeared to be illustrating the label being used.

4

A Summary of the Three

Before we continue on with the technique, it seems appropriate to incorporate the three previous chapters into a single summary. You should have, at this time, a pretty good idea of what goes into making up a character for portrayal. If during the exercises you have stumbled in the class level of characterization, it's not necessarily bad. It only goes to prove that you simply needed work on the level, whichever level it was. If you had trouble with the labels and dialogue, that is alright too. Regardless of which of the three chapters you may have found trouble with, it only indicates that you should simply practice them. With practice will come the ease of movement, or the truth of the lines and the labels. There you will have isolated the need or problem that you had. Now you simply work on the solution to the problem. What is of greater concern is that you understand the need for breaking the character down into functions that you can deal with.

It is the theory behind this technique that you must understand. If you understand it, then you can effectively put the "tools of the trade" at your disposal; with these tools you bring your talent to the set, and that is where it counts. With these tools you are no longer operating in the dark. As a result, there is a great reduction in the nervousness you would have experienced.

The nervousness can never really be eliminated. That will be with you as long as you are in the business. I know actors who have had fifty years of stage and screen experience. To this day, they are nervous before they go on—whether it's the stage, screen, or radio. Once they begin, however, the nervous energy is properly directed and the performance is again professional. So the case of nerves which I'm certain all of you have, is nothing to be concerned about. You just have to learn to direct that energy through your choices. Use nervousness to your advantage, for the energy level must always be up.

As was stated in the sensory chapter, your nerves may make your performance rigid. Many actors I know are very good, but it takes them too long to warm up. In the theater that may be acceptable, but definitely not in film. It is your responsibility to be prepared when you go to the set. Your performance must be loose, and the control and knowledge of your character must show through your sensory responses. Loosen up before you rehearse the practice scenes. Breathe deeply, and stretch your muscles. Shake your hands as they hang limp from your sides, and roll your head clockwise, and then counterclockwise. Also, breathe deeply. All these things will help you loosen your joints, so that you can work within your characterization much more freely.

One very famous actor merely walks to a corner of the set and "psychs" himself up. Sometimes it takes five minutes; other times only a few minutes. I have seen him work a scene where he actually did no "psyching up" before we shot. It probably had something to do with the type of character or the scene. His style of bringing his energy up does not work for me. With me it's primarily breath. But I do loosen the body. Before I am at the studio, I have done the following: spoken lines from Shakespeare, shouted, stretched, walked, rolled my head, and shook my hands damn near out of their sockets. Those are my ways. I hope they work for you. I know that several of my friends use the same technique to loosen up, and that is why it was chosen to be included in this book. Whatever works for you, do it! The loosening-up exercise is merely a point from where you can begin. I perform loosening-up exercises the same way before an audition as I do before a performance.

The loosening-up exercises cannot be overstated because they will help your body respond to your mind much more gracefully, and your mind will function much more clearly. Explore the different ways that it takes you to loosen those joints; it may take a while.

In making the choices for an economic level I have a few suggestions. The problem sometimes arises that the actor is not familiar with the economic level that he is to perform in, or he hasn't performed in it for quite a while. Therefore, the choices don't come to mind that easily. Well, you have the perfect subject for study at your disposal, and that is you. What do you find bothers you in other people? Is it low class to take out a handkerchief and blow your nose? Do you? Would you? Is it low class to have your blouse or shirt not neatly tucked into your skirt or trousers? For you? This comparison can, and should, be carried from economic level to sensory responses. Do you smoke when you are nervous? Would the character? Would you comfort your senses in the same manner as the character? How? If the character is of the same economic level as you, the choices may fit exactly what you would do. If so, then use them. If you use mannerisms that are yours alone, and the scene calls for a response that you would not give, then you must make a different choice.

If you are portraying a character that fits your particular habits and way of life, don't hesitate to utilize those habits. Many actors are reluctant to do this, because it seems that they feel they will be criticized by their peers for "not acting." Do not allow yourself to fall into this syndrome. I believe that the reasons for the rejection of this syndrome should be obvious to all actors but apparently they are not. The first and most obvious is, of course, that your performance will be very natural. It is this very naturalness that the audience can relate to. They will believe your performance. Isn't that, after all, what we are out to accomplish? Other actors are quick to criticize this type of acting by saying that the performer is not an actor but rather a personality. Again, you must remember that as an actor you bring to a role a piece of your personality, your individual imprint. You will perform in a role only as you can do it. If you attempt to imitate other actors, you will end up as one who "looks like," or "sounds like," or "acts like" so and so. When it comes time for you to be considered for a role, you will not be thought of as a unique talent but rather as the shadow of some other actor. What the industry needs is some variety in the actors, so that if some producer or director or casting director is looking for variety in a role, they will call the actors they believe are individuals. Consequently, those actors that imitate successful actors must necessarily wait until those whom they are imitating cannot do that role. And even then the best you can do when you are imitating someone is be as good as they are. You can never top them, so retain your personality. Make your mark on that role you are playing. That role can be a one liner; it makes no difference. There are no small roles, just small actors!

The idea of your individuality carries over from the economic levels to all other aspects of the character you are to play. If some successful actor portrays a role that you now have to play, try to avoid playing that role by imitating his performance. That does not mean, however, that you cannot utilize something from that performance. It may be a little bit of business or some other minor aspect. That, I think, is valid because it's like doing your homework on the character. But what you do borrow from the other actor should be fashioned to your personality. You will make your character breakdown as was outlined. If you find that the character should have some quality or habit that was used by another actor, then by all means use it. However, use it your way. Blend it into the choices, and rehearse it at home. If it works, then use it!

The choices for the economic level are quite clear. Actually, most of the time the choices are obvious, but there will arise, on occasion, a mixture of levels. A role may have you performing in a high class economic level rooted in a low-class background. When you begin to rehearse your character at home, and by yourself, take comparisons from your own behavior. Now, the character is high class, so how would a low class person appear high class? Don't forget our character *is* low class, and that character would have some flaws in his high-class image. They are not really obvious flaws, but ones that would show up under conditions of pressure or pleasure when he is not entirely in control of his reactions. This puts us into the sensory and mood labels. In acting this character out, you should make choices that appear under certain conditions. These choices would be true indications of his background. The reverse would be true for a high-class character who has become an alcoholic, or maybe a tramp or an artist who has decided to change his way of life. This character also would give away his true background if you made choices that you display under certain conditions. Perhaps you could mix the choices by having the high class character walk in that manner, yet have the choices for his personal habits indicate the class that he has fallen into, or risen from.

The mixture of choices in developing your character is accomplished by using the tools that this technique provides for you. These tools are not ends in themselves. On the contrary, they are a means to an end. When you practice the economic levels, the sensory reactions, or the labels for those moods, you are becoming familiar with those tools. You shall become so familiar with them that you can act them out in different shades or degrees. When you practice them, you should take them to the extreme. If the label is "tears," then bring tears. Sometime in your career you will have labeled a scene in which your character is so disturbed that he is on the verge of tears—so much so that the character must fight to suppress them. In a scene such as this, you would label yourself to tears, then fight to suppress them. So, the importance of knowing how to be broad should now be obvious to you. When you know that you can reach them and you have demonstrated it in your practice sessions, the unknown begins to disappear. In place of the unknown, a sense of confidence will appear. It's all in knowing what to do and when to do it. Though many of your performances in the practice scenes will initially appear mechanical, do not despair, because you are developing your technique. All of us can do these labels when we are ourselves under conditions that bring those labels out, because of our own feelings; that is instinctive. However, at first they will appear stiff because they are conscious choices. You are not operating by instinct. Gradually you are developing a control of these actions. So you can see that the more you apply these choices in your scenes the more familiar you will become with them, and the more natural they will seem to the audience.

Another thing that you should do while rehearsing your practice scenes is to *cut it in half*. By cutting it in half, you should not lower the energy level. You bring the physical reactions down but keep the energy up. So it is your movements that you bring down, and that includes the facial expressions. In a master shot, your facial expressions and physical movements can be fairly broad. However, in a medium shot those movements appear larger because the camera magnifies everything. In a closeup, a facial expression that appears normal in a master shot will definitely seem like mugging. Mugging is o.k. in certain situations, because it happens in real life. However, unless it is a choice, it is not correct. Remember, do your scene according to your choices for the master shot, cutting your movements in half for your medium shot; for the closeups cut them in half again. Use your mirror at home. Take a look at yourself while you go through scenes 1M and 2M, and you'll be surprised to find that what you thought was very broad is, in fact, not recognizable as that label. At other times, what you think is normal you will find could be considered "mugging." What you must look for is a balance between the two extremes.

If you are practicing the exercise scenes by yourself, see if you can find a kindred spirit to be your audience. This person is to perform two functions for you: one is to call "Action" and "Cut"; and the other is to *measure* your labels and choices. They are not to comment on the esoteric, as the esoteric has no place at this point. When you have command of the tools, this might be all right, but only then can we comment on the esoteric. At this point you are to convince your audience of the labels rather than have your audience say to you, "Yes, I believed, [or] I understood what was happening to you." Or, "No, I did not." Have your audience measure you by giving points to each label.

For example, suppose you choose to perform exercise scene #1. You are to utilize all the sensory responses, and choose an economic level of low class. After the performance your audience would then rate your sense level from one to ten. Say that in conveying the sense of smell you left no doubt as to what you were doing. At this point your audience would give you a ten. However, in the economic level, they did not understand, therefore, they would give you a zero or one or two. If your energy level is down, then you would receive a numerical rate for that. Consequently, you can get a breakdown of your needs; this is only to help organize yourself in application. The lower numbers that you receive are only for the labels and utilization of a sense that you have not sufficiently performed. The higher numbers are given not for being broad but for being convincing. You communicate the feeling or label, and you get a rating for that. Being broad aids you in finding your limit. And you can, if you choose, continue to be broad in your performance. Remember, *your* imprint is on that scene.

Your friend should begin your action and end your action. You are not to stop once the action cue is given. If you feel yourself fumbling, continue on. Recover while you are doing the scene, and try to blend the fumble into the scene as best you can. But do not cut the scene yourself. This is very important because on an actual shoot, you may be performing your scene and you may stumble somewhere within it, but the other parts of the scene are okay. Well, the director can cut that piece of film in the editing room, and still use the rest of the scene. He can replace the gaffe with a pickup, or he can make a dissolve. There are any number of things that he can do, but all these things that can be done with that film are for him to decide, and not for you. If you cut the scene, then you have taken over the director's job. There are many classic scenes that exist today on film that were actually mistakes, but the actors blended those mistakes into the scene, and the final result was better than the intended result. Since this technique is patterned after the actual manner of shooting in Hollywood, you are to apply yourself in the exercise scenes as you would on a "hot set," and you should do this right from the beginning. When you do your homework for characterization, then you are in command. Once that action cue is given, you must act!

When you are performing the scenes with the dialogue (scenes 1M and 2M) your friend—substituting for the audience—should call the cut for the scene at varying times after the dialogue has been completed. You have performed your opening label, spoken your lines, made your transition to your other label, and there hasn't been any word from the director. In this instance, you should continue acting within your closing label, and stay in that label. Do not end the scene as the scene is ended when you hear the word "cut." The time between your last word of dialogue and the call for cut we shall call "director's" time. Many times, the director will like what you are doing within a particular scene. He may have in mind a way to use your performance to emphasize an emotion, or to extend the film in time, or to use it as a pickup in some other scene that was fumbled. To do this, he must have you performing until he calls "cut." While you are performing your label, and after your lines have been completed, he may have the camera zoom in on you, or zoom out on you. This may be something that he did not discuss with you before the scene started, because he had no idea that what you were doing would be so good or so convincing that it gave him an idea while you were performing. Rather than cut the scene and discuss it with you, go with the spontaneity of the moment. After he calls, "cut," he may then discuss it with you and decide to recapture what you had done. These are the unexpected changes that occur in filmmaking. These are the little creative bits that put an actor in demand in Hollywood. They put him in demand because they mark him as a professional. It is common for an amateur to end the scene himself because he fumbled a line or completed his dialogue. In the first instance, he brought attention to his fumble by stopping the scene and in the second instance, he did the director's job, and indicated that his performance did not extend beyond his lines. In both instances, I am certain that you can see the error of those approaches. There probably will be times where the fumbling gets too bad for you to recover, then the director will cut and start the scene over. After all, he is watching your performance. If you happen to have forgotten a line, then try to paraphrase your dialogue. If they cut the scene, then you should call for the line. There will be a script girl there to give it to you. It has happened to me, to actors with whom I've worked, and it has happened to actors with whom I've spoken. Those instances will probably occur with you as well. But the thing that you should do is continue on as best you can until the word "cut."

Don't think that fumbling a scene happens only in dialogue, or that it will always be your fault. There will be circumstances on the set that may have nothing to do with your performance, or the performance of the other actors. It may be that props will fall, or something will float by your field of vision while you are performing. It may be that a prop is not set in the proper place for you at the time you need it. You may save the scene by looking for the prop, or ignoring the floating object, for instance. The important thing is that you continue; don't get rattled! This applies to commercials as well as T.V. and features; in fact, *All* film making. It is that important to you and to your career. So, in these practice scenes, for all intents and purposes, you are on a hot set. So treat it that way and function that way. Begin on action and end on cut.

In performing the exercise scenes 1M and 2M, you should mix the labels as much as you can. I suggest though that you confine yourself to scene 1M until you really feel that you can call on the physical manifestations that show the labels convincingly. Scene 1M contains six lines. Within these six lines, you have made your transition from opening label to closing label. Try making your transition on a given line; then try doing it between lines. Also try various timing combinations within those lines, and vary the labels. When you have difficulty with a label, don't avoid that label, work on it. I have found that the label "tears" is one of the more difficult ones for men.

In reaching the label "tears," I haven't any fool-proof suggestions—although some actors go so far as to pull the hair in their noses! There is a less painful way that may work for you, so try it. Think back into your life. Find something that happened to you, and try to recall how you felt, then try to physically repeat it several times. By doing this, you may be able to work out a pattern that will bring tears to your eyes.

After you have some degree of control over your labels in scene 1M, then you should begin scene 2M. In this scene, you have eight lines. The reason for the increase by two lines lies in the third label. You should be able to handle the opening label and the closing label. Now don't get them mixed up, and make the transitions clean. Make the transitions clear enough to be read by the audience. Don't keep it inside of you, but let it all hang out. Keep that closing label going after you have ended your lines. All your scenes are to begin with the idea that they do not end with the lines. So the label is carried on. Any recovery of a fumbled scene should be in the label that you had going at the time of the fumble. Do not change the label for the recovery. You must stay in whatever label you are in until you make the transition to another label. This means that you must concentrate on that label.

This brings us to the focusing of the energy. The scattering of energy will be spotted by the audience, even though they really don't know what it means. To you, the actor, it means that you are not taking the audience to the point of the scene in which your character is performing. If your lines are directed to some object that had been the possession of a person you loved dearly (and you are speaking your feelings to that person through that object) then speak to that object as though it *were* that person. It is essential that you direct your energy to that object. When you do this, your audience will go with you. When you say your lines in scenes 1M and 2M, you say them according to your label, to some focal point that you have in your mind. Interpret those lines according to the label, and when your label changes it does so completely. This doesn't mean you make the transition abruptly all the time, for you can build up to it—but it must be complete. If it is abrupt, make it clean and clear. When it is not abrupt, make the gradual changes clean and clear in levels and that can be played as effectively as the abrupt transitions. You will get the feel of it, and it is called "timing." Timing is part of that individual personality imprint that you are to bring with you to the set.

All these exercises that you have performed have been done with no other actor in the scene. Soon you will become capable of becoming involved with one, two, three, and even more actors, as well as working lines, labels, sensory, economic levels, and blocking. I know you're anxious to get to that part, but be patient and practice your scenes. You see, in film acting, you must be prepared. You must perform under many different conditions. You must perform effectively with or without other actors in scenes that are identical, but with only you on that screen, so it is essential that we concentrate on you. And then, of course, there are the commercials. We certainly cannot neglect them, as they can provide handsomely for you. In commercials, you will probably be working alone most of the time, regardless of whether it is a local, regional, or network spot.

In commercial industry, you have to sell yourself at the audition just as in film work, but there the similarity begins to end. The immediate demands in commercials overshadow the demands of film. Primarily, it is because there is so much less time you have on camera. In situations such as these, this technique will serve you well. How does an actor create a character in thirty seconds? Use the technique!

In answering the question above, I will have to undertake a round-about approach. In commercials it is not so much that you create a character, but rather that you put a standard character into a situation for thirty seconds. Advertising usually doesn't want any economic level other than middle, so you will usually find yourself working in that economic level. The variety will come with the sensory responses and label. The character habits will have to be changed and applied for different commercials. The character habits should be keyed to the type of work that the character does. On one commerical you may be a farmer, the next, a man who owns a small contracting business and on another, just "plain Joe," who does not indicate what kind of work he does. So the breakdown of habits would be put under sensory reactions, because when they describe the occupation of the character you are playing, it goes something like, "He's a truck driver." or "He's a small businessman." Your choices can be made by comparison. The choices you have applied to characters played in films can be applied here, with the sensory reactions and label focused on the product.

At the audition, you will have demands thrown at you that you had no idea could come from the script you have. As an example: just recently, an actor I know had an audition for a large retail department store. The store was having a sale on a national brand item used in a car. This could have been a good commerical financially, even though it was a sale item. This actor has very few film credits, but some stage credits. He also has worked as an announcer. He told me the lines that he read and the way he read them. It was a direct pitch to camera. As an announcer it was a good reading, but when he got into the audition room, the director said to him, "You are in your own garage working on your own car, and a friend of yours walks in and you say your lines to him." The actor was unable to even come close. His reading was unvaried in style. Why? He had no idea at the time, or even later, how it could be done. If he had applied technique, he would have had a chance. With technique you break it down. You're in your own garage . . .(*sensory reactions*) . . .working on your own car (*sensory*) . . .and a friend comes in . . .(*label*) . . .and lines to friend concerning product . . .(*label*).

For sensory, you would bend over to show that you are working on your car. You would look up when friend walks in and smile. Apply an opening label of Joy—after all you just bought a product on sale at your favorite store, and you're proud of it—focus your energy and wing it. Now you could have done it that way. And you may say to yourself, "He's second guessing that other actor." No, I am not. The breakdown I just gave you is a very superficial one, and I brought only three choices into it. No doubt, with some time to really work on it, any one of us could come up with more. For example, one could wipe dirt from your hands, moving towards your "friend," who, by the way, is not there! So you see, there are innumerable choices and ways to do it; it is not just a pitch to camera. Many producers of commercials that I have talked to about actors and auditions, and related subjects, have all expressed a common denominator on the subject. They say that many of the actors they have auditioned have never varied their characterization; consequently, it isn't really necessary to audition them over and over again.

There should be no reason for an actor not to be able to come up with several different ways to portray a character—even if the scene is thirty seconds long. It's a matter of making choices and knowing where those choices are coming from, and why they are made. The people that are auditioning you might not like the way you audition. They may say to you that they didn't see the commercial that way. They may ask you why you did what you did, and you can tell them that you had made choices, and that they were based upon concrete thinking. When you are able to discuss choices from that level, and not an arbitrary point of view, you will see a different attitude from those people. Even if you don't win the audition, you may rest assured that you will be called again and again by those people until you get a job from them.

I hope that you see the application of these tools of our trade. I have tried to explain their application in film, TV. . . . . and in commercials. This technique is designed for the film industry. It is designed for you, as an actor, to function within that industry with every available advantage to display your talent. The production people and the crew are all there to help you do your job. Understanding your craft is your responsibility. You will be hired not only because of your personality but because of how well you can act.

You now have the first three of the applications. From this point on you will still function alone in front of the audience, but the functions now will concern voice, delivery, and the styles of delivery.

This book is not one concerned with the technical aspects of speech and speech delivery. That is a subject in its own right in which you learn the basics on different deliveries. Here, I will present some exercises you can do to loosen your voice, and make it sound natural while delivering your lines. These you can do before rehearsing your exercise scenes.

The application of what you have learned in the previous three chapters is to be incorporated into the next phase, so that you will perform under the direction of the demands to be presented to you now. Whenever you perform from now on, you will make conscious choices. While you were performing the exercise scenes 1M and 2M you should have noticed that the way you labeled the scene had a bearing on the way you said the lines. The lines were nothing more than nursery rhymes, yet they could be delivered with different meanings, so it is not so much what you say as the way you say it. The way you say the lines is influenced by the labels, the economic choices, and the sensory choices.

The goal of all this is to get you to be able to do these things smoothly. You can accomplish this! If you practice. Practice . . .it is what makes you familiar with the things on your conscious level that you do instinctively. When you can do them on the conscious level, then you can repeat what you have done as many times as it takes to get the scene filmed. If you try to function by instinct alone, the outside influences must be reshot, or if the scene calls for pickups, then all outside influences must be identical. That sounds much too difficult to me. How about you?

5

Dialogue and Delivery

The voice is the prime method of communication. For an actor it is essential that he keep it in top shape. You must know how to deliver your lines with sincerity and believability when you are speaking into a microphone. You must learn to pace your delivery. You must learn to match your previous delivery.

On the set of a television show or feature film, you will find that your delivery will closely follow the labels that you have chosen for your character. The sensory choices will influence your delivery almost automatically. The choices of sensory and mood changes that you practice actually will *aid* the delivery. The voice merely has to be used in practice sessions that are designed for the delivery of lines. You have that in scenes 1M and 2M. However, that is not enough by itself. The voice should be used in different types of dialogue. By that I mean when you are loosening up your voice in the mornings or afternoon or whenever, you should recite poetry, or passages from Shakespeare—anything that will give your voice a range exercise. The exercise should include these because it will make you pronounce your words with a more conscious attitude.

The pronunciation of the words and the pace of delivery are indications of the class of a character. A middle- or high-class character has a different delivery from that of a lower-class character. The pace and pronunciation also can show what part of the country the character is from, or from which country for that matter. So when you speak lines from Shakespeare, and you make them believable and understandable, it will help you in contemporary delivery. You may never play Shakespeare, but it will still make you think about the way in which you use your voice. As in the sensory reactions, your senses will respond to your delivery. And conversely, your delivery is influenced by your sensory reactions. Hence, if you stand erect, your head high in a pose of some aristocrat, your delivery will begin to take on the tone or manner of an aristocrat. It is all within the sensory reactions. When you practice a delivery, take on the physical attitude of that delivery. It will help you in the lines.

In the commercial industry the voice-over business is a big one. If you decide to enter into this field I strongly recommend a coach, a good voice coach. He can guide you in the art of announcing. This is a craft in its own right. The actor should be able to play the part of an announcer. But the announcer is not expected to play the part of an actor. So you see that as an actor you must develop your voice to a point where it is pleasant and not strained. The audience must not be able to detect strain in your delivery. If it does, it will not be able to identify it as strain, only as unpleasant. Barring any physical ailment, everyone has a good voice. It can be made pleasant to listen to by the way in which you speak. This can be accomplished by the pace at which you speak, the phrasing you use, the tone, and the volume. Speaking into a microphone as a commercial announcer, or a voice-over person, you learn the technique of using the microphone as an aid in delivery. Sometimes your mouth is very close to the "mike," other times it is not. I mention this, not to tell you the technique of voice-over, but only to bring it to your attention that the microphone is part of a voice-over person's method of operation. When you practice voice-over on a tape recorder, you can apply that. And if you must make choices someday when you play the part of an announcer, then you have one already.

The copy that is used for voice-over in television commercials and many radio spots is, many times, difficult to deliver. It is designed to get a message across in a given amount of time. The copy has as few words as possible with the most amount of information about the product. It is the job of the voice-over person to make it sound pleasant and interesting—and all in that given amount of time!

The voice-over people that I know have applied a technique of timing the script. What they do is mark the script for pauses, for modulation, and for accelerations. This is a visual aid for the performer. When they go into the audition they can speak the lines with more sincerity, because they do not have to think about the delivery. They can put meaning into the words. The eye triggers the speech for the technical part of the delivery. As in acting, the preparation that performer goes through is the element that determines the difference between success and failure.

The marks that usually are used for pauses that you wish to make between phrases are one line for a short pause, and two for a longer pause. These marks are placed where you think the phrases should be broken up. The phrasing as well as the voice quality is what determines the person that the ad agency will hire for the job. As far as the voice quality is concerned, you can manage that by moving the microphone closer or farther from your mouth.

For the voice modulations you can use the marks... for raising the voice and... for lowering it. When you get to short connecting words you can use the mark... This would show that you speak right over those words. It is these words which you use in shortening your delivery time. You can skip right over connecting words and get to the words that actually mean something to the commercial. If your delivery is running short, then you extend the time you speak the connecting words. It should not be construed that you do not say the connecting words or that you slur them or speak them so that they are not understandable. No, it is that you do not spend time on them. Words like *it* and, *is* are considered to be the connecting words. The mark for words like that would be placed beneath the words. The beginning of the mark on *it*, the end of the mark on *is* ... example... it, and is, When your eye hits that mark you would automatically gloss over those words. The marks for modulating the voice would be put over, between, and under the words that you have chosen.

"When it is cold outside... wear Jones Long Johns." I marked that line only for an example. You may see it another way. I hope so—that is what makes the business. Do it your way. Make that individual imprint.

A good way to test your growing ability in voice-over is to try to read newspaper ads out loud. These ads are not designed to be spoken. They present a real challenge. As in reading an actual script, you should ignore the punctuation. The punctuation is for reading, not for speaking. Your marks on the script are what you deliver by. Many actors make the mistake of reading punctuation especially at auditions. For your own information, take an ad and read the copy with punctuation. Then with the same copy, mark it and read it without the punctuation. I am sure you will find a pleasant surprise.

If you can get your hands on a tape recorder, do it. Use the recorder for practice. Experiment with the microphone to find what distances are needed between your mouth and the mike for the different effects that you can achieve. Your goal is to achieve a naturalness in your delivery.

When you deliver lines as a voice-over person, you are talking to people through the microphone. But you are talking to people. When you deliver lines on camera, you are talking to people through the camera. There is an obvious difference. You can not stand there like a stick and deliver your lines, because the viewer is looking as well as listening. So when you work on-camera, use the sensory and mood applications. Watch yourself in the mirror when you are delivering the lines from a newspaper ad. Do not be afraid to animate. If you naturally move your face muscles in certain deliveries, do it. That naturalness is a great selling point, both for you at the audition and for the product on the job.

As an actor you will be called upon to give several types of deliveries. I am not speaking of moods. I mean different kinds of monologues. Identifying them is as it was with everything else in this business: the first half of the job. So I will identify them for you. They are used in the film industry as well as in the theater.

Soliloquy:

The actor is actually alone and talking to himself. This is a dramatic monologue that gives the illusion of being a series of unspoken reflections. In films you would probably do the voice-over this scene. But you would act the scene out first. Onstage you would speak the lines but give the *illusion* of *unspoken* reflections.

Narrator:

The actor recites the details of a story. He talks directly to the audience.

Dead Air:

The actor speaks his lines to imaginary people. He gives the illusion of their actually being there. The difficulty here is that you have no one to give you responses, and you must rely on your own energy. You will be in this situation often in films. This occurs in filming out of context, as well as in scenes where you are speaking on a telephone or to someone in another room.

In Scene:

The actor has others in the scene with him but he is doing the lines.

These are the different types of monologues with which you will be faced. They occur onstage and they occur in the films. The application of these monologues begins with the sensory reactions and the labels. The practice exercises in the previous chapters can be utilized perfecting them. The labels you choose will have a direct effect on your delivery in these monologues. They are not difficult after you have practiced them.

In auditions it is important to have made a choice in your delivery and be able to demonstrate that choice to the people for whom you are auditioning. The mood and sensory choices, of course, will aid you in the delivery. But the skill in the delivery will weigh heavily in your favor. Think back to a scene that occurred between Richard Burton and Peter O'Toole in the film *Becket*. The scene was a conversation between the two as they sat in chairs. They appeared very comfortable and interested in what was being said. But the delivery was made from a sitting position, and the scene was a fairly long one. They managed to hold the attention of the audience with their delivery. This type of acting is what this chapter has been about. A good delivery does not make you an actor, but it is certainly essential in acting, and it must be treated as a separate tool. The days of the moody, mumbling actor have past. Now people want to know what an actor is saying, and they *want* to believe what he is saying.

I know that this chapter has described more of the commercial application for the voice. That is because there is a more technical approach to that field. In acting, once you have made your choices, you will be able to get into the scene, and when you do, your voice modulation and inflections will follow. But what you *must* do is to practice that voice so that when you speak you speak clearly, and with feeling. And above all, do not try to change the quality of your voice. Let that remain. So many people think that because they do not own a golden set of "pipes" they cannot become an actor. Nothing could be farther from the truth. What an actor does do with his or her voice is to control it.

He has it at his command to sound pleasant and to keep the interest of the audience through the audience's sense of hearing, when that is needed in the scene.

Many actors' workshops pay little attention to the voice. This, I believe, is totally unfair to the actors. Since it is the job of the performer to convey to the audience the ideas and story that the author has created, it seems essential that it would be primarily through speech. Words are our most important way of communicating ideas. The way in which we say these words communicates the mood of the speaker, and although it is only one of the ways that an actor can get ideas to an audience, it is a very important one.

When you practice with the dialogue for voice-over, or when you speak the speeches from Shakespeare or poetry, you are giving *your* voice a range. You are becoming familiar with your own ability to talk. People who are not actors probably do not realize how little they do talk. And when they are speaking it is usually in short sentences. Then, also, they are speaking their own thoughts. So they come to the point. When they see a piece of paper in front of them with the thoughts of another person written on it, with long sentences that include the mood the author felt for those thoughts, they panic. That is why the art of acting is a discipline, and not many people will even attempt it. But it is not frightening when you understand what you must do to be able to say the thoughts of another person with the feeling that keeps the interest of the audience. And what must you do? Get familiar with your own ability. Learn to control your voice, and you will be able to recite from Shakespeare with the same ease with which you speak your own thoughts. You will begin to discover that you have an individualism in delivery. Your phrasing may be different or the tone you use for certain phrases. This could be yours. Or maybe it is the sound of your voice. There are many actors who achieved a great deal of fame by the way in which they delivered lines or the way they sounded. I do not think it is necessary here to tell you who they are.

There was a famous mimic who, on his own television show, said that, since the stars of the Thirties, there are not too many people for him to imitate in the film and entertainment business. He said that so many actors try to be the same that if he imitates only one he has covered the field. I did not invent that remark, but it fits into my belief so comfortably that I remember it.

However your voice sounds, capitalize on it. It is yours. If you learn to control it, you are in business. Deliver your lines your way within your sensory and mood choices. Convince the audience of what you are saying. *Make* them believe you. If you get the idea across to the audience, you have done your job. Nobody can say that you are a bad or a good actor, only an interesting one or a boring one. Make your line delivery interesting. It was said that the late Charles Laughton could read a railroad timetable to an audience and make it interesting. Maybe we will never become that good, but we can damn well try.

When you are speaking your lines to another actor, whether in a scene or at an audition, watch that energy level. A pitfall that you will very often encounter is matching the level of the other actor and not performing within your choices. What happens is that one actor will set the energy level in delivering his lines and other actors follow. This presents a problem to an actor who wants to function on another level. You may feel the scene slipping down in energy. What you must do to bring your delivery up is "step" the energy level back up. If your delivery is too different from the other actor, when you speak your responses to him you may lose the mood choice. This pitfall, then, reflects on you as well as on the scene in general. I have seen television shows where the lead opened the dialogue with his particular style or delivery, which was to underplay the role. Now, that was very effective—for him—but what happened is that every actor in that scene began to speak his lines on that level. The scene was flat and dull. Even the actress in the scene was on the same level. When she spoke her lines she gave the impression that she was imitating the lead, as was every other actor in the scene.

This pitfall is particularly dangerous when you are auditioning. To counteract this and still maintain a logic in the scene, you step the energy up by beginning your lines on the level of the other actor. And then within your lines you bring the energy level up. By the middle of your delivery try to have reached your level. But begin your delivery at his level—then step it up. If the difference in energy is too apparent, it can leave some big holes in the scene. By stepping up the energy level in your delivery, you make the transition from low to high nice and smooth. The same with the reverse: if the other actor is too high for you then you step the energy level down. This helps you to keep your character individual in the scene. If the other actor begins to take from you and stays at your level, that is his problem, not yours. You maintain the level that you have chosen for the scene. When you feel yourself slide into his or her level of delivery, begin your stepping up or down of the energy level. Do not wait. Do it as soon as that sameness begins to appear.

The danger exists particularly at auditions. In the next chapter you will find out why it exists there in particular. The energy stepping must be applied there.

6

Auditions and Cold Readings

Now we are in the area of "make it or break it," for it is here that you must convince those who are watching you of your ability to perform the part that you are there to win. As important as this phase of the business is, it is ironic that it is this phase in which you have less time to work the part out and do that with the least amount of information about that part. True, you will be given some information about the character, but the fact remains that, if the people who are auditioning you knew exactly what they wanted, they would book that actor who could perform the part to their specifications. So at the audition you can safely say to yourself that there is something they are looking for in the character that is yet unidentified.

At this point you have at your disposal a set of tools that you can utilize to create something for the character. But the audition itself presents a set of problems of which you should consciously be aware. You use the tools, but the time you have spent on the lines usually is relatively brief. That means you will probably have to read from the script. Your eyes must follow the lines, both yours and those of the person with whom you are reading. Now your attentions are divided. How do you apply the character choices: Suppose the person you are reading with has a low energy level. Suppose the lines are delivered to you in such a way that they carry no meaning. Perhaps the person with whom you are reading does not look up from the script. Suppose the person with whom you are reading is not an actor.

Each and every one of these situations will occur at auditions, mostly because, in Hollywood, the auditions have you reading with the casting director. Of course, sitting in on that audition are the producer, director, writer, and sometimes the associate producer, and maybe a relative or two of any of those people involved in the production. The auditions in Hollywood are much the same as those you will experience in other parts of the country. They have the same features that you must overcome when you audition for industrial films, educational films, and, in many ways, commercial films. The one thing that actors newly arrived in Hollywood usually do is to be overwhelmed by the fact that it is Hollywood. That has some merit, however, because you are auditioning for people who have worked with the best in the business. What you have in your favor is that they are looking for something that has not yet been found. If you can impress them with your professionalism, you are in business.

When you first arrive at the audition you will be given the script to study. You will be told the scene number and the character. From here on you are on your own. The director and producer probably will choose a scene in which the character you are to play displays a range and depth. If it is a day job for which you are auditioning, then it is the scene that you will work. In the beginning the day job is what you will probably be doing most of. So let us begin there.

First of all, read the entire scene. Look to find out where the scene takes place. Read the lines that the other actor or actors have. Try for the "feel" of the scene. Try to determine the attitude that prevails in the scene. Is it high energy? Low energy? What is the point of the scene? After you have worked out a general idea of the scene, then read the lines of the other actors and your lines. But your lines you speak out loud. The first few times you say your lines, just say them. Get familiar with the words. Say them as many times as needed for you to get comfortable with them. After you have decided that you have spoken them naturally, then begin to apply your choices for labels and for sensory reactions. Now, when you have made the choices for your character, apply them to the lines of the other actor. In the case of auditions, you usually will be reading with someone who is not an actor. So you must have your ear turned to the line for a reaction. The casting director with whom you are reading will probably put nothing into the lines, and it is up to you to listen to his lines and trigger your responses to the lines and not to the reading. Apply your choices when you hear a word as well as an entire line. If you have decided that the scene is an intense one, then you will be intense. Look the casting director in the eye (if you can get his eye; if not, then look at the top of his head or whatever he presents to you). Keep the intensity until your next choice comes up. When he reads his line to you, it is at a low energy level. I do not know whether or not this is intentional, but it has been my experience that it invariably occurs. When it does occur, step the energy up from his level to yours. It is a bit difficult at an audition, but remember that they know that. You are not expected to hit it on the button right then and there. What they do want you to show them is how you will perform that scene. If you step the energy level up gradually, then the reading will be smoother. A difference in energy levels can work against you if it is too wide.

If the scene involves three actors and the casting director is reading the part for two of them, then before you start reading, ask if it is all right to have you place the other character in a location. Then pick a spot on the wall or a piece of furniture and when you speak to that character, then you direct your gaze there. In picking the location, make certain that the people in the audition can see your face while you are delivering your lines to that character. And make that location favorable for you. Try to pick the place that shows your face in its best light.

The reading of the lines must be as smooth as you can make them. If you are a quick study, then of course you will memorize the lines. Believe me, I envy those who are a quick study. I am not. I have to refer to that script all through the cold reading. There is a method that has been developed over the years by many actors. It has proven its value to me many times over. I use my thumb!

At the audition, since they want to see you act as well as speak, you have to have a way to get to your lines once you have taken your eyes off that script. The thumb! As you progress through the lines, keep your thumb alongside the lines that you are to deliver. You will have become familiar with the lines, and once your eye picks up the first few words of your next line, the entire phrase will come to you. When your eye hits that line, you are to ignore the punctuation just as you would do for advertising copy. Phrase those lines within *your* character. If you happen to paraphrase a line, *do not* stop. Continue on. If your paraphrasing is within the concept of the scene, it may not be noticed. If it is not, you will be asked to read it again.

Once you have begun to read, do not permit yourself to be rushed. Pace yourself, but maintain that pace. If the pace is quickened by whomever you are reading with, step it down. Whatever choices you have made, stand by them. If you permit the other person to control the pace, then you will probably lose the job. If the choice that you have made is an aggressive one in attitude, then be aggressive, and try to vary the aggression in degree. Your character will be one of three attitudes, aggressive (forceful), neutral (will stand not flee), or withdrawn (will back off). When you have read the lines of the other actor and you feel that your character would withdraw his aggressions on certain lines, then you must display that, even though the casting director or whoever else reads the lines flat. When you get to the words the other person is delivering, that will trigger one of the three attitudes in your character. Pick it up there and wait for your cue word and deliver in that attitude.

The character you are reading for may have all three of the attitudes in that scene, but you may see only one or two. If your reading is interesting enough, then the producer and director will discuss it with you after you have completed your reading. They will then tell you what they feel. If those attitudes in the character are what they want, do it again. Ask them for a moment to think about it. They will give you time. Then apply the three attitudes broadly. If they think it is too broad, they will tell you to read it again like that but bring it down. Many times the director will ask you to change the attitude of that character several times, and ask you to read it several ways. Do not let that bother you. They do that to see how well you can take direction. Do not get rattled if the change that they ask for is how you reacted to the request. If you rattle, then when you are on the set and the scene has been changed you may get rattled. And when you are on the set money is being spent every minute. If you are calm and can handle change, you will not cost the producer any extra money. They like that.

The producers and directors like when an actor comes into an audition with choices for a character. They like it even more when the choices are delivered smoothly. The smooth delivery of choices comes from practice. The smooth delivery of choices comes when you get familiar with the words in your script. Say them out loud as many times as you need before you go into that audition. Use your thumb or finger to keep you on those lines. Know where your reactions are going to be according to the dialogue of the other actor. Trigger your reactions to those words or lines in his dialogue. Be broad in your reactions. But try to make it appear natural. Breathe deeply before you go into read. Loosen up your muscles. This will help you to relax. We all have a case of nerves before we go in.

There is one more thing that may sound a bit insignificant, but nevertheless, it is very important to you. Do not socialize! You will find that at most auditions you will be running into old friends that you have not seen since the last audition. They will tell all about the parts they are "up for." There will be all kinds of small talk and nervous energy pervading the room. Stay away from it. You are there to win a job. There are certain things that you must do before you go in to read. We have just discussed it. Do the things that you must do. If you have to, go to a quiet corner of the room or outside and read your script. Do your loosening up exercises, get familiar with your lines. Make your choices. Walk through the part, if that helps you. Stand, sit, walk—do whatever you want. But lock your mind and attention on the part. I know personally of many auditions that were lost only because the actor did not go into that reading prepared. You have little enough information to begin with. Do not reduce that with idle conversation to your fellow actors. Socialize after the reading. Then it will help you to work off the energy you have built up. Besides, everyone will be talking about the way they read. You can pick up a lot of good tips on characterizations and cold readings from them at this time. Exchanging information after the audition is not at all bad.

The auditions that you will go through for the commercials have only a slightly different approach. You will recall that earlier we said that the producers of the commercials want a middle-class character for their products. This works in your favor. When you read for these auditions, your choices do not have to come from a large base. The base from which you will find yourself operating is usually the same because of the middle-class person that always uses the product you are in the commercial to sell. The only variation you find is in the character's occupation.

With the knowledge that all you will have to vary is the choices in character occupation, we can safely assume that the commercial producers and directors are going to buy— you—your personality—the way you do things and say things. I do not want you to think that all you will have to do is walk in and they are going to leap up at you and say sign here. No. Not that at all. You will still have to put effort into winning the audition. The things that you apply to winning theatrical auditions are applied in commercial auditions, also. However, the difference between the auditions is that you deliver your lines and your action in a much more limited scope. You go into a theatrical audition expecting to read with a casting director and display your choices in the lines he reads to you. In commercial auditions the casting director does not read with you. If there are more actors in the commercial, then you will be paired up by the casting director before you go in to read. The pairing up, whether man and woman or man and man or woman and woman, or any of those combinations along with children, animals, or products, is made by the casting director from composites.

When you walk into a commercial audition you are there because you are a type. But the type is middle class. Actors feel that if they are not the current fad type then they are not commercial. Nothing could be farther from the truth. Size, weight, etc. bear an influence on the choice that the producer makes, of course, but the physical appearance is not all they look for. I, myself, won an audition for an on-camera pitch where the original idea was to have the person in his fifties with grey hair and the lined face of an outdoor type who is an ex-Marine. I was fifteen years younger than the average actor who auditioned, smooth faced, and I am an ex-soldier, and I am losing my hair! So you see, the idea that the agency people have about the commercial can be changed as far as the on-camera people are concerned. As I said, the type you try to be is middle class. There is the key. The way that middle class people dress and act varies, but only slightly. If you are a hippie type, then what you do is go to your commercial auditions dressed and acting like a middle-class person—which may not be too far from what you really are. But if you are an actor, it really should not be too difficult.

Many of the decisions in casting a commercial are based on appearance. That is inescapable. After all, if you are selling cars that you claim have a lot of leg room, then you do not want to hire an actor who has long legs—right? The same is applied to diet products and sodas and so on. Appearance does have an influence, but it is not all. When they are casting for an entire family, family appearance is important. But they must start somewhere—with the father or the mother or the children, but somewhere. So if you impress the producers enough, they will begin to create a family from your appearance.

The scripts that are used in commercials are very much different than those used for theatrical films. It usually is composed of one sheet. The sheet is divided into two, with the dialogue on the right and the action on the left. The camera shots are included in the action. The action is designed to fit the lines. For example: You may have a script that calls for you to look at a bowl of cereal while you are saying you are not going to like it—then a shot of you tasting the cereal and your expression changing from doubt to enjoyment—then a shot of you smiling with the spoon in your hand and saying you are in love with the product—than a shot of you looking admiringly in the distance saying to your wife how wonderful she is for discovering this product—the shots are synchronized to your lines. This will show on the script. But when you go into the reading you will be asked to do the entire scene without the cuts and changes. When you look at the dialogue you will see breaks in the copy to correspond with the action. These breaks are sometimes so large that they appear to be new paragraphs. To deal with the copy that is written in this manner, you apply yourself as you would with voice-over copy: ignore the punctuation and the breaks in the copy. Characterize your delivery. Phrase that copy your own way. Blend it together.

In your delivery you must focus on something. In the theatrical auditions you had the casting director. Here you have no one. So to help you make your delivery natural, pick a focal point. At that point put in your mind some imaginary figure. Then speak to that figure. Speak directly to it. And speak the entire copy while you perform the actions called for in the script. Focus on one thing at a time. If our example were to be your audition, then you would have picked a focal point for the wife *before* you begin your action on the bowl of cereal. Then you focus on the cereal as you speak your lines. Apply the sensory responses for taste as you begin to change your label, and then bring your focus to the point that you have previously picked and deliver your next line to that point. You do all this within one continuous action. The only breaks in the delivery would be the phrasing that you make, and for the action of the sensory responses. There are to be *no* breaks in the delivery of your sensory responses or in the mood changes. The mood changes are to be smoothly delivered from one label to another unless otherwise called for in the script.

The time that you take for your performance will be determined by the length of the commercial. On almost all of the scripts you will find in the upper left hand corner the length of time that this commercial is to run. It may be a twenty-, thirty-, or sixty-second commercial. This time that you see there is the time for the finished product. When you are auditioning it does not determine for you how fast you will deliver. For the audition and for you it indicated how many choices you will throw into it. Do not try to time the commercial audition. And *do not* rush through your delivery, any of the deliveries, dialogue, sensory responses, or label. If your delivery is much too long, then they will tell you to speed it up. You then may shorten the delivery time, but even when you shorten it by reducing some of the choices, do not speed up the important choices. Eliminate the unimportant ones. Speed makes things look unnatural, and you, as an actor, must deliver your performance in a manner so natural that the audience will believe what is happening to you. At the audition the audience is the producer, director, and other agency people. The first impulse that actors have is to impress the agency people that they can deliver their lines within the time shown on that script. Well, I have a bulletin for those actors—the time shown for the length of the commercial is for the *finished* product, which does not necessarily mean your performance. There are tag lines, logos, and a multitude of other things that are included in the finished commercial. So at the audition you think in terms of delivery within a reasonable time that is called for. But the important thing is that you must be able to perform the action smoothly. That is what they are looking for.

In delivering your performance here you should always keep in mind that for commercials the delivery should be broad and the energy level up. At the auditions the agency people as well as the director seem to like the very broad delivery. So give it to them broad. And when you deliver your lines to camera keep a smile on your face. If the smile is not required, then you can remove it, but even then, keep the smile in the eyes. This goes for any delivery that you make other than those in which the choices call for something else.

The delivery for an on-camera pitch is in a way similar to the voice-over for timing. But the energy level at audition has to be kept up even though you have nothing off of which to bounce the energy. When you go into the commercial audition it is all up to you. So you must practice on-camera delivery to your mirror many times. Then when you deliver at the audition, you will have an idea of what you look like in manner and stance. Of course, your labels and sensory responses will help the delivery where you are a character, but in the straight pitch, where it is just you in a suit talking to that camera, you cannot stand there like a stick that talks. The best thing you can do here is to be yourself. You have the ability to speak well; you know how to deliver those lines. You can make it interesting by being yourself. There is nothing wrong with individuality, especially in commercials, and in the film business in general. So be yourself, but keep that energy up. You know how to do that. So even if you feel rotten, keep the energy up and deliver as though you do not feel rotten.

Perhaps it will help you to understand just how broad the commercial auditions wanted the actor to perform by studying the ones that are currently running. Turn the sound down till you cannot hear it, then watch the action of the actors. Study them individually, especially those whom you think are doing parts that you feel you would get. But do not ignore the others, because they all have something to offer and utilize.

The auditions that I have discussed here are of two types: theatrical (film and television) and the commercials. You will find that all auditions fall into those two categories. The film and television industry is growing at a phenomenal rate. This growth rate also includes industrial films, training films, educational films, short spots on local television stations—there are so many that it would take a chapter by itself. Each industry is realizing the value of the film industry in promoting its product or increasing the efficiency of its production. This is not to mention the increase in motion pictures and the voracious appetite of television. So when you audition and win the job, and then perform in front of a camera, then do it as you would do it in Hollywood. When you come to Hollywood you will find that your auditions and your performances are a lot more relaxed. It is because you *are* a *film* actor. The work you do on stage is a great help to you. The stage is an art form. I enjoy working the stage. I am sure you do to. But the two are quite different in application, as I hope I have shown so far. I do not wish to give the impression that I am suggesting a film career over a stage career. No. I am trying to acquaint you with the tools that you will need, even if you are an experienced actor.

Hollywood is the film capital of the world. Let there be no doubt about that. I have worked in Rome, and there I was treated like visiting royalty because I came from Hollywood. Because Hollywood is big and getting bigger, and because of the television industry, it is a very confusing place to the newly arrived actor. There are agents, casting directors, both for theatrical and for commercial films, there are studios, production houses, and television stations. The major motion picture studios, the large ones, the small ones. Who is what? And where? What is an independent casting director? What is a staff casting director?

In the chapter to follow I am going to try to explain to you how it all fits in. In other words, the following chapter will be the first one that introduces you to Hollywood and to the film industry. What you have had thus far is what is expected of you, the actor, at the audition. What is expected of you on the set. What the demands are that you will face in becoming a working film actor. You were given the technique that works for me, and has worked for innumerable actors in the past. And it will work in the future. Whether you use it or not is entirely up to you. If you choose to use it, I hope that you will apply it as an individual. I hope that you will keep your individual imprint on your performance while utilizing the technique. Hollywood does not need two of every kind, as Noah did. It needs individuals.

Practice is what you need as an actor. When you are not working, it is a good idea to join a workshop. The tools of the trade get dull, as they do in any other trade. So if you have not worked for a while and you feel you have mastered the technique of film acting, then go to a workshop and sharpen up those tools.

When you audition for a film—regardless of what type of film it is—regardless of where the film is being produced— do it as you would in Hollywood. Apply yourself to a safety film or religious film or industrial film the same way you would on a feature film in Hollywood. Do not vary that in your career. Be as professional in the small-town production as you would be in the big-town production. No job is small and no part is small, there are only small actors.

CONTINUED:

And as Holbrook reaches over to show her we TIGHTEN
on Cort, frowning, and

                                          CUT TO:

EXT. LOCAL TELEVISION STATION - DAY

As we MOVE IN, TIGHTENING on the call letters, while:

                    ANNOUNCER'S VOICE (OVER)
          ...This is K___-TV, your community
          service station, bringing God to
          Bakersfield...

INT. LOCAL TELEVISION STATION - DAY

ANGLE - DIRECTOR'S CONSOLE, its battery of televisions
all brightly lit with various angles of a talk show-like
set for what we hear as:

                    ANNOUNCER'S VOICE (OVER)
          And now, live, we bring you
          the Susan Cort Misson First
          Annual Prayerathon. To tell
          us more about it, K___-TV presents--
          The Reverend Susan Cort!

As the announcer speaks we're WIDENING to show the
control room activity, director and other personnel
hard at work. The director flicks a switch, and instead
of the religious motif card with the Susan Cort Mission
name on it which has been there, his main monitor shows
the area where, under the announcer, the country-western
band has been playing a hymn both rousing and holy. The
hymn is nearing its conclusion as the camera on the band
pans to another area, where Susan sits on one of several
chairs arranged in a semi-circle. A cross is prominent
behind her, but there are no other religious signs as
she looks directly at us, starts to speak, and we:

ANGLE - SUSAN

Because we're with her now instead of seeing the image on
camera we also see the cables, wires, other camera set-ups
around the young woman. She seems oblivious to them all,
speaks slowly, calmly, smiling in a way that shows she
is really quite serious--and that nobody else in the
world has ever been more sincere.

                    SUSAN
          Thank you for joining us. Tonight
               (MORE)   (CONTINUED)

*The following are examples of typical scripts you will be working
with as a film actor. The first example is from a script titled
"Messiah". It is a film script written by Larry Brody, the supervising
writer for Columbia Pictures. The story line is about a large corpo-
ration that decides to get into the religion business.*

CONTINUED:

                    SUSAN'S VOICE (OVER)
          Oh, Councilman, excuse me.
          They're telling me its time
          for a look at the new total--

INT. LOCAL TELEVISION STATION - NIGHT

ANGLE - TOTEBOARD, where the figures are moving,
changing, stopping at the proper amount, as:

                    ANNOUNCER'S VOICE (O.S.)
          The new total is--one hundred
          fifty-four thousand five hundred
          and sixty-seven dollars--and
          eighty-seven cents!

ANGLE - SUSAN

With the announcer and the man we know must be COUNCILMAN
MILLAR, while the band plays another fanfare. Susan's
reaction to the amount is that of a little girl filled
with delight. She claps her hands, turns to the camera.

                    SUSAN
          Thank you everyone...

                    MILLAR
          It's a pleasure to be part of
          this worthy effort. I've often
          said--

He would like to go into great detail, but the announcer
looks off, turns back to Susan, overriding:

                    ANNOUNCER
          Susan, excuse me. But we have
          another talented local performer
          here today, a great supporter
          of yours. In this, the ninth
          hour of the Susan Cort Mission
          Prayerathon, we are proud to
          present--the Amazing Mr. Collingsway!

He gestures, and a man in tails comes dashing out,
rolling a table before him. He's a magician, one
of those who works without words, and as the band
plays his music, the Amazing Mr. Collingsway goes
right into his routine.

*Note that the dialogue in the scenes is continuous, but the script
calls for different angles to be shot of the performers during the
scene.*

ANGLE - HALLWAY

Where Holbrook and Cort stand behind all the newsmen,
watching Susan. They speak in low tones.

                         CORT
             I should be with her. That's
             what being her husband's all
             about.

                         HOLBROOK
             Jonathon, the fact that Susan's
             married makes people see her as
             'safe.' But the minute a husband
             turns up with her for something
             like this--any wife looks like
             a puppet.

                         CORT
             And Susan can be nobody's--
             'puppet?'

His voice holds just enough irony to make Holbrook
certain it's there. The young man is chafing.

                         HOLBROOK
             Look, John--whatever you might
             think, Susan's handling this
             just right. Just as she's handled
             everything else.
                     (beat; lightly)
             And with ninety-five percent
             of the newsmen out there working
             for publications or stations
             we own, what could go wrong?

ANGLE - SUSAN

Before Cort can respond, another question coming over
the others being asked.

                         MAN'S VOICE
             Mrs. Cort? Mrs. Cort?

                         SUSAN
                     (finding its owner)
             Yes?

WIDER ANGLE

As the MAN who spoke crosses from the front door.
He's middle-aged, seemingly middle-income, speaks
quietly...but with what amounts to great passion.
                                        (CONTINUED)

*Note that there are demands placed on the character in the role of
"Man" . . . . Economic Level-Mood Label.*

CONTINUED:

                    MAN
          Mrs. Cort, I don't have much.
          Work down at the hardware store,
          on Fifth near Hawthorn. But
          if the Mission needs it--every
          penny I have--it's yours.

Both Susan and the newsmen are equally startled,
and the others turn to see who this is.

                    SUSAN
          I'm sorry--what was that?

                    RENTZEL
          Sir, are you a member of the
          press?

                    MAN
          I'm a member of the Mission.
          Been wherever you've talked,
          Mrs. Cort, ever since I saw
          you the first time, couple
          months ago. When I heard you
          were talking today--I had to
          be here.

                    SUSAN
          I'm very flattered...

                    MAN
          I thought, if there was anything
          I could do...so others'd know
          about you...You changed my life,
          I mean it.
                    (beat; to newsmen)
          She did. She told me that God
          understands. She told me He
          forgives. Since I heard her I
          don't feel guilty anymore. I
          can live with myself--because
          I know God doesn't blame me for
          all I done wrong...

His voice is building as though he's putting himself
into his own sort of ecstasy. Rentzel looks around
frantically, trying to figure out what to do, while
the newsmen listen, smiling, cameras training on the
man, knowing this is the best copy there is.

                    RENTZEL
          Sir, please, this meeting today
          is just for the press...

                                        (CONTINUED)

CONTINUED:

>   MAN
>   (through increasing
>   hubbub)
>   I just wanted you to know, that's
>   all. Susan Cort's way isn't just
>   the best way for men to live--
>   it's the only way. She's not
>   just another preacher, she's
>   a prophet--
>
>   RENTZEL
>   (desperately)
>   Sir...
>
>   MAN
>   No, no, no...she's more than a
>   prophet. I don't care if she
>   is a woman. She's the Messiah,
>   for sure. She's the Messiah...

And, still thinking about it, pleased that he's groped
for and found the right thought, the man suddenly looks
around, realizes all the attention he's getting, the
laughter he's causing. He whirls, frightened, rushes
out. One newsman hurries after him, another, another,
at least one camerman, calling after him, AD LIB, while
the noise level among those remaining continues to
increase.

ANOTHER ANGLE

For all practical purposes, the press conference is
a shambles. Rentzel crosses to Holbrook and Cort,
his face a furious mask, Susan coming after him.

>   RENTZEL
>   (an angry hiss)
>   Dan, what the hell's the matter
>   with you? Ringing in somebody
>   like that can ruin everything
>   we've worked for.
>
>   HOLBROOK
>   Mike--I didn't 'ring in' anybody.
>
>   RENTZEL
>   Then whose idea was that man?
>   Adams--?
>
>   HOLBROOK
>   I'm telling you, he was nobody's
>   (MORE)   (CONTINUED)

UNITED AIRLINES
60-Second Film
"ERNIE"
PASSENGER SERVICE
UAPA9420

Approved for Bidding: 3/26/76
Revision #1: 4/15/76 dm

VIDEO	AUDIO	
1 ERNIE DROPS BOLT IN, CONNECTING PLANE AND HIS TOW TRUCK.	SINGERS:	TAKIN' CARE ALONG THE WAY ......
	SFX:	CLANK (ECHO)
2 STEPS BACK, CLAPS HANDS.		CLAP, CLAP (ECHO)
3 WHISTLES BIT OF UNITED TUNE.		WHISTLE (ECHO)
		THROAT CLEAR (ECHO)
4 PICKS UP WRENCH, PRETENDS IT'S A MIKE AND GIVES A BOARDING ANNOUNCEMENT.	ERNIE:	Ladies and gentlemen ... United Airlines Friendship Service flight seven forty-seven is ready for boarding ... complete with our roomiest comfort, finest cuisine, and friendliest crew ...
5 HE ACKNOWLEDGES ECHO OF HIS NAME WITH HIS ARM.		and it's all brought to you by yours truly, Ernie Hammil. (ECHO)
6 HOPS INTO TRUCK.	SINGERS:	SPREAD A LITTLE FRIENDSHIP, LET IT SHOW, WATCH IT GROW ... (SFX: START)
7 DRIVES OUT AS HANGAR DOORS OPEN.		FEEL IT CATCHIN' ON NOW, EVERYWHERE YOU GO
	ANNCR:	At United Airlines, friendship is an energy, a spirit that reaches all of our people.
8 SHOT OF ERNIE DRIVING, LIP-SYNC WITH SINGERS.		Even those you never meet.
	SINGERS & ERNIE:	COME ALONG SING THE SONG ......
9 DRAMATIC SHOT OF TOW PULLING PLANE.	ANNCR:	That's why we're the number one airline in the land. The better we feel about us, the better you do. (JET SFX:)
10 ERNIE LEANING ON TRUCK, WAVING TO HIS PLANE, TAKING OFF.	SINGERS:	THE FRIENDLY SKIES
11 MOVE IN.		OF YOUR LAND
12 747 IN SKY. SUPER LOGO.		UNITED AIRLINES.
	SFX:	WHISTLE TAG AND ECHO

orm 5-44 6/73

This is an example of a commercial script. It was provided by the Leo Burnett Advertising Agency. Note the difference in the script structure. The Video side of the script (left) describes the actors action in the commercial. The Audio side (right) describes the pre-recorded singing, the sound effects (SFX), and the dialogue of the actor and the announcer (voice over). Note that there are no demands in this type of script for the role of Ernie. You must get this information from the casting director, or the people conducting the audition at the time you are auditioning.

```
UNITED AIRLINES
TV :60
"ERNIE"
3/26/76
```

WRITER'S PRODUCTION NOTES

CONCEPT: To portray the likeableness and spirit of all United people through one...Ernie Hammil (his name for now)...the guy who drives the tow truck that pulls the big planes to the ramp for boarding.

CASTING: Just one. Middle aged Ernie. A guy you gotta like a lot. There's some Walter Mitty in him.

SCENES: A scene by scene story is on the stats. Here is the story of this commercial.

Ernie, the guy who tows the planes is in a giant hangar with a United 747. He is in the process of hooking up the plane to his tow. The sounds he makes, like the clank and the whistle, are echoed throughout the big hangar. This gives him the inspiration to pick up a wrench as a mike and make his own personal boarding announcement to no one in particular. As he reaches the end of the announcement, his name continues to echo through the hangar. And he gives a politician-type acknowledgement as he steps onto his tow and drives the 747 into the light. There is some voice over singing...although Ernie lip syncs to part of it.

Then we dissolve to see him leaning against his tow, looking up to the sky waving to his plane which has just taken off. As we see the plane rising in the sky, we hear the whistle that Ernie gave at the beginning of the commercial, echoing back as we fade out.

TRACK: Could supply a scratch track for timings, since there is some singing and whistling...and one line of lip sync singing.

ANNCR: Burgess Meredith, post recorded.

Jack Smith

/saw

WRITERS PRODUCTION NOTES. This is what the writers had in mind when they wrote the commercial script. Note the demands of the character "Ernie", they are Mood Labels. *Also note that no economic level is made; that is assumed by the writer. The actor never gets to see these notes.* Courtesy of Leo Burnett Advertising Agency.

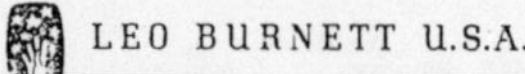

LEO BURNETT U.S.A.

PRUDENTIAL PLAZA   CHICAGO, ILLINOIS 60601
312-236-5959

UNITED AIRLINES
10-Second Live Television Billboard Tag
for "HAWAIIAN OPEN" (ONLY) PROMOTIONAL TAG
BILLBOARD

Client Approved: 12/23/76 dm

THE FOLLOWING LIVE TAG COPY IS TO BE DELIVERED EXACTLY AS WRITTEN
IT IS NOT TO BE CHANGED IN ANY WAY WITHOUT CLEARANCE FROM THIS AGENCY.

LTV-1921-PASS-BB-10

VIDEO		AUDIO
SLIDE #757: YOU'RE THE BOSS BUTTON AND UNITED LOGO.	1 ANNCR:	... United Airlines. Fly the friendly
	2	skies of United, where you're the boss.
CHANGE TO SUPER SLIDE # 'O 'OE KAHAKU BUTTON AND	3	Or, as they say in Hawaiian,
UNITED LOGO.	4	" 'O 'OE KAHAKU".

*This is an example of a voice over script. The announcer is not seen
by the viewer of the commercial.*

 **LEO BURNETT U.S.A.**

PRUDENTIAL PLAZA · CHICAGO, ILLINOIS 60601
312-236-5959

UNION 76 DIVISION
60-Second Recorded Radio Announcement
"TIME IS MONEY"
TRUCKSTOPS

As Recorded:
Typed: 1/29/76 ws

<u>01135-TK-60</u>

1   SONG: ROLLIN' DOWN THE HIGHWAY
              COUNTRYSIDE SLIDIN' BY
              YOU GOT MILES TO GO, HAULIN' THAT BIG LOAD
              WISHIN' THAT YOUR BIG RIG COULD FLY

2   ANNCR: Time's important when you push a big rig for a living! You try <u>not</u> to

3   stop more than you have to, and when you <u>do</u> stop, you want to make

3   every minute count. That's why a lot of drivers always look for Union

4   Seventy-Six TruckStops and Auto/TruckStops. They're places where you can

5   save a lot of time -- because you can probably get everything you need <u>all</u>

6   <u>in</u> <u>one</u> <u>stop!</u> Fuel and service for your rig ... a good old-fashioned

7   "stick-to-the-ribs" meal ... a place to shop that's open twenty-four hours

8   a day! And at most locations on the Interstates, you can even get some

9   sleep and a hot shower! So if time's important to you, plan to stop at

10   Union Seventy-Six TruckStops and Auto/TruckStops -- and take advantage of

11   "One-Stop Convenience!"

12 SONG: TAKE ADVANTAGE OF US. THE SPIRIT OF SEVENTY-SIX.

These are examples of radio commercial scripts. Note that the length of the commercial is in the upper left corner, the same as with the TV commercial script.

LEO BURNETT U.S.A.

PRUDENTIAL PLAZA · CHICAGO, ILLINOIS 60601
312-236-5959

UNITED AIRLINES
10-Second Live Radio Tag
for "WEST COASTERS"
PORTLAND

Client Approved: 1/30/76   dm

THE FOLLOWING LIVE TAG COPY IS TO BE DELIVERED EXACTLY AS WRITTEN
IT IS NOT TO BE CHANGED IN ANY WAY WITHOUT CLEARANCE FROM THIS AGENCY.

L-3206-PASS-10

1   ANNCR: Fly United's West Coasters to California. Four daily nonstops to

2   Los Angeles. Nine to San Francisco and the Bay Area.

LEO BURNETT U.S.A.

PRUDENTIAL PLAZA · CHICAGO, ILLINOIS 60601
312-236-5959

UNITED AIRLINES
60-Second Live Radio Announcement
"CALIFORNIA GOLDEN SEALS" (POST)
WESTERN DIVISION
PASSENGER SERVICE

Client Approved: 1/5/76   dm

L-3166-PASS-60

1   ANNCR: Now's the best time for you to spend a little free time -- and save a

2   lot of money. With United's new Freedom Fare. Because now, you can save

3   thirty percent off regular round trip Coach fare. And fifty percent for

4   children under twelve traveling with you. There are no mileage restrictions.

5   No holiday or weekend restrictions. You're free to leave any day, and

6   go almost anywhere. Just pay for your round trip ticket within ten

7   days of when you make your reservation - and no later than fourteen days

8   before your departure. Stay seven to thirty days. There are a specific

9   number of Freedom Fare seats set aside on most flights, so it's a good

10   idea to make reservations early. United's Freedom Fare does not apply

11   to flights within the same state or to Canada. There are different

12   discounts available to Florida and Hawaii. And remember, on June first,

13   the summer discounts begin with smaller savings. So why not save now

14   and stay home later. Just call your Travel Agent. Or call United for

15   information about specific Freedom Fare cities and flights. Now's the

16   time.

Part II

THE BUSINESS

7

Agents and Casting Directors

When the average actor arrives in Hollywood he has a multitude of questions in his mind. Some of the actors know someone who has been out here, or is still here. If you are one of those actors who knows someone out here, then you are a step ahead of the average. But you might as well read this anyway, since you've gone this far.

The first questions, of course, are: "What about an agent?" "How do I find one?" "What do I have to do when I get one?" The first one is probably not too hard to figure out. However, to those of you who do not know, you get a list from S.A.G., that is, Screen Actors Guild. It is located in Hollywood at 7750 Sunset Boulevard. If you are starting out cold, this is the best bet for you. They will provide a list and you make your pick from there. S.A.G., however, will not make recommendations either of agents to you, or you to agents. They stand neutral in that respect. They also do not classify them as good, bad, or indifferent. The top agents in town are well-known to the people in the industry. There is no way you can tell the top from the bottom by looking at the list. You will have to find that out by asking questions of people in the industry.

The agents in Hollywood, around the country for that matter, are franchised by the Screen Actors Guild. These agents are the only ones that you should deal with. It is through these agents that the legitimate film industry works. There are some people in Hollywood especially, who pass themselves off as agents, but unless they are franchised through S.A.G., I would not consider them as agents. S.A.G. keeps pretty tight reins on the agents. A lot of the hanky-panky that the film industry is accused of does not happen through the franchised agent. It happens through those who claim to be agents. If you are ever approached by someone who tells you that he is an agent and he will work for you, good. Do not start a question-and-answer period with that person, about whether or not he is legitimate. Instead, you listen politely, take his card, and tell him you will stop at the office at your first opportunity. Then if you have any doubts, go over to the S.A.G. office and check him out. The people at S.A.G. are more than happy to assist you.

When you get the list, you will have to begin calling the agents. This can become a long process. The agents usually keep a set number of actors in their "stable." The top agents especially are difficult to get to see. But you must call anyway. Sometimes you will talk to the secretary and some-times you will talk to the agent. But unless you keep calling you will not see anyone.

Some agents operate with only a phone and an office. Others work with an entire staff of subagents. That is to say, one person has the franchise for the agency but has hired other people to go out into the field and drum up the work for the actors. It is the larger agents who have the subagents working for them. You may hear of some "agent" who is really hot in Hollywood and yet he is not listed with S.A.G. That means that he works for an agency who is listed. Whatever he accomplished for the actors whom he represents is credited to the agency for which he works. His business card will include the agency he works for as well as his own name. So, in actuality, he is not an agent, but a subagent. Some of the really large agencies represent not only actors, but writers, directors, producers, and other related crafts-men. These agents are called packagers. They are the people who have a larger staff of subagents. If you are directed to an "agent" who is not listed, all you have to do is ask which agency he is with. Then you can check.

If an agent operates with only a phone and an office, that does not mean that he is small. Some of the really big ones are one-man operations because they choose to be that way. What they do is restrict their "clients" to a certain number of people. They usually will not take on new clients unless they feel that they have an opening in their "stable." The number that the agents keep is not really large. They will keep the number proportionate to the number of "types" they feel are moving. The size of the agency is not the criterion for picking the agent.

There are agents who are known for having only the power to get day jobs for their clients. I really could not give the names of those here because I do not know them. Agents I know of have clients that have running parts on weekly television shows, and yet actors I have talked to say those agents represent only day players. On the other hand, there are some very big agents who have friends of mine as clients, and the friends of mine complain that all they get are day jobs. So you see, small agents and big agents seem to be in the same ballpark. It must be the actor who determines how big his parts become!

The agents in Hollywood try to keep their field of operation either in theatrical work (television and film) or in commercials. So when you sign with an agent for your theatrical representation, you must find an agent for your commercials. Sometimes the theatrical agent will try to have you sign with him for commercials also. That decision is up to you. But I have found that what works for me is two separate agents. The commercial agent makes many more contacts in that field than the theatrical can do. Each is a separate field, actually. The actor must act in both fields, but, businesswise, they are distinct.

When you sign with a theatrical agent you have a head shot made into a composite. On the back of the composite you will put your résumé. The agent can help you in picking a photographer to take the pictures. The photographer to whom he sends you is probably the best for you at this time, because he knows what the agent is looking for in the style and type of picture. After the pictures are taken, they are put on a contact sheet. That means that they are all on several sheets in small frames. When you get your contact sheet you will take it to the agent. He then picks out the shots that he thinks best for your composite. The style of each composite, is usually a full head shot on one side, and maybe one or two small head shots showing different attitudes on the back side. The shots on the back side would be printed small enough to allow for your résumé. On the front side is the name and address of your agent. The agent then has you place your picture in the Academy Directory. Many times the agent will see that the picture is placed in the Academy. But in either case you pay the fee. You also pay the photographer, and the printer of the composites. These are your costs. They are all necessary. The Academy Directory is like the Bible of the industry. The casting directors refer to that constantly. The composites are what the agent submits to the casting directors when he thinks that you are right for a part.

Now with the commercial agent you will run into the same procedure. But the composites are different. The commercial agent must have a larger selection of photographs of you on each composite. With the commercial composite your pictures should be of you in a more broad portrayal of 'types." You would have several selections of wardrobe in the composite, each selection intended to show a different type of person. Here again it is usually best to have the agent make the selection of the photos, as well as the photographer. On the commercial composite you do not put a résumé. The entire composite is of pictures of you with the name of your agent on the front side. Also there is no Academy Directory for you to be placed into. So that expense you do not incur with your commercial agent. As with the threatrical agent, you pay the expenses for the photographer as well as for the printer.

The difference in the composites is the reason that you cannot use one composite for the two agents. The theatrical pictures show you, full face and well lit. The casting direction then can see just what you look like. Your readings and acting are the closing of the job. With the commercial composite, the casting director must try to match you to other actors for very short exposures, and in different occupational attitudes. Your reading and acting are, of course, very important also. But the different wardrobe and poses help that casting director in mixing and matching. So you see, as with everything in the film industry it all boils down to business, time, and money. Your composites are designed to save time for the casting director.

The theatrical agents subscribe to a service called a "breakdown service." What this does is give the agent a wider scope for submitting his clients for different jobs. Years ago the agent had to go to the studios and read the scripts to see if there were any parts for his clients. That took a lot of time. The service has the characters in all the shows being shot broken down to what part they perform and generally what type of person to play the part. The agent receives these breakdowns almost daily. Then he makes his selection for the part from his file. After the selections are made, the agent delivers them to the casting director of that show, who is also listed in the breakdown. The agent then makes an attempt to see the casting director to sell his client to him.

When you are a new arrival in Hollywood, the agent will make appointments with the casting directors for a "general" interview. The general interview is necessary for the new arrivals even if they are well-known stage actors. It applies the same to them as it does to inexperienced actors. The general interview is designed to acquaint the casting directors with you personally. The agent considers this a very important meeting for you. The casting director considers it very important because he can expand their files of actors for the different shows they are casting. The casting director does not audition you at the general interview. Instead, he more or less studies you. *You* are on display. The conversation is around you and your background. The casting directors of the three-camera shows usually like to hear that you have had stage experience. This is probably because of the fact that the shows are shot in front of a live audience, and in sequence. Not that film casting directors do not want to hear about stage experience, but the film people seem to consider it more or less as simply training.

The casting directors are reluctant to give large parts to newcomers, even with extensive stage credits. This, I believe, is because of the difference in the techniques between the two. This reluctance is what you should try to quiet down in the casting director at your general interview. When you are speaking of your past experience, include the stage credits, the film credits, and the commercial credits. Talk about the workshops you have attended, or are going to attend. If you have not made plans to attend a workshop, say so to the casting director, but qualify that by asking the casting director if he or she can suggest one or two workshops to you when you feel the need to sharpen up your tools. If you have a workshop in mind, tell that to the casting director, then ask if he has heard about it. Explain why you are interested in that workshop. Explain it in the jargon of the industry—"It's good in developing characterizations" or "It's a film workshop," etc. The point is, you should try to impress the casting director with your professionalism, not your ego. The casting director will see hundreds of actors. Each one will display the ego, but what the casting director is looking for is professional actors. So that first interview is important to you to be seen as a professional.

Casting directors also like to know that the actor is working. So if you can get into a "showcase" theater, it would be wise to mention that you are in one or you are "up" for a part in one. This does not mean that you should spend all your time in showcases. On the contrary, you came to Hollywood to do films, not stage. But in the interview the casting director wants to know that you are professional enough to work at your craft in all aspects. Also, it will serve to quiet the doubts he may have about you by showing that other people in Hollywood are willing to hire you.

The film credits you tell the casting director about may not impress him if they are not Hollywood film credits. Do not let that get you down. The Hollywood people consider their productions as the top, and rightly so. The result is that they tend to look down a bit on films that are not done by Hollywood, but you have to start somewhere. If you give an air of confidence, and speak with the jargon of the industry, you will begin to work, small at first, but with the tools you now have, you will build up and up. The casting director may intentionally say things to you that are designed to rattle you, so do not get rattled. Remember when the casting director hires an actor it reflects on him directly if that actor does not come through. So he must, of necessity, be careful about the actors that he chooses. This includes the actors that are called in for auditions. The professionalism must be carried through by the actor from the minute he or she hits Hollywood. No. From the moment that you decided to become an actor. If you came in an audition and did not appear to know what you are doing, this would reflect on the casting director, to the director of the film and the producer. If your audition is well done and you still do not get the job, it reflects well on the casting director, because he is able to get qualified actors to read for a part. So what it means is that the casting director wants to save time and embarrassment by having general interviews.

During your interview you should be "up" in your energy—not to a ridiculous point, but to a point where you are alert and attentive. Try to be yourself, but with a good energy level. And for heaven's sake do not try to emulate some successful actor. Hollywood is looking for individuals!

When your agent gives you the time and date of your general interview you will want to talk to him about the person you are going to meet. You can be a lot more candid with your agent. Whatever you can think of before the interview, ask your agent about it. If you can think of nothing, then say that to your agent. It is just as important to the agent that your interview be successful as it is to you.

As far as the commercial casting directors are concerned, you will not have any general interviews. The commercial casting directors function as free-lance agents to the production companies. They do, in most cases, maintain an office, but do not hold interviews for talent. They rely more on the agents to provide the people for them directly at the audition. Your agent will undoubtedly send you on auditions, at the beginning, that you believe you were entirely not right for. This is because the agents feel it is important that the casting director get to meet you. And this is the best way for you to meet them. It may sound awkward for you, but still you will have to go along with it. Like everything else in the film industry, the commercial agents do the things that work best and most efficiently for them. Whatever works for them will, in the long run, work for you.

There is one more thing that your theatrical agent may set up for you. That is an audition scene. Some of the major studios will have their casting directors set aside one day every so often for these audition scenes. The entire staff of casting directors will watch scenes performed by the new talent in town. They do not ask for a particular scene to be performed. They leave that to the discretion of the talent. The only regulation that they place on the talent at all is of time. The time limit is three minutes. The scene should not run more than three minutes. I have known of scenes that were cut by the casting directors while the talent was still performing. This is not because the casting directors are unfeeling or ruthless; it is because they have scheduled other auditions for the day. And they can allow only so much time for each audition. So you see even when you are just breaking into Hollywood, the word *time* is a key element in your approach to success.

The audition scenes that are set up by the studios give the new talent in town a good opportunity. At the audition scenes you will find all the casting directors of that particular studio. The major studios maintain a head casting director, and a staff of casting directors. The staff casting directors are assigned to the different weekly shows for television or other films that are being shot there at that particular studio. So when you have a general interview with a casting director, it exposes you to that particular show. But the audition scenes expose you to all the casting directors of the studio, consequently to all the productions that are being shot there.

There are free-lance casting directors who will become staff for a particular production company. These production companies will rent office space on the lot of a major studio and will shoot their production through the facilities of that studio. But they function independently of the studio. So their casting people are not related to the activities of the casting directors of the studio. The casting people of these productions your agent will make appointments with. This again is the general interview.

The major television networks also keep casting directors on staff. The offices and studios are scattered all over Hollywood. Here again, although the networks keep the staff of casting directors and shoot their own productions, you will find independent shows being shot through their facilities. The independent productions will have their own casting people. If you have an interview with the casting director of one of the networks, you will still have to see the casting people of the different independent shows. And if you see some casting director that has an office on the lot of a major studio or network, it may not necessarily mean that you have seen the staff of the studio or network. Your agent, of course, will probably tell you who is who when you got to the lot, but it is up to you to know the way things function in Hollywood.

The general interview and the audition scenes are your introduction to Hollywood. It is here that you first meet the casting directors. It is through the casting directors that you meet the directors and the producers. And it is through the directors and the producers that the public meets you! The public is the final judge. They are the ones that accept you or not. Once the public has accepted you, you are on another plateau in the film industry. The casting directors no longer have to be concerned with whether or not you can perform the part. They know you can. You now can see why the technique exercises are designed to get all the emotions and lines to the public, and why the rating system is fashioned to whether or not you displayed what the demands of the scene called for. The technique plays down the esoteric portion of the art until you control the tools of the craft. When the casting directors interview you, they are listening and watching with a professional eye. They know consciously and instinctively that the actor is required to perform out of context of a scene, without the aid of other actors—and all of the other demands the film acting places on you.

At the general interview the casting director will listen to you to satisfy himself that you are an actor, and that you are capable of film acting. When you speak in the terms of the film actor you will help to quiet doubts that the casting director has. Speak as a professional actor and you will begin to get calls for auditions. At the auditions—perform. Apply the technique. Create characters—be interesting. Think about the role you are to audition for. Make choices, and, above all, retain your own personality. Stay an individual. Do not try to be the carbon copy of whoever is successful at the time. Keep in mind that it is the casting director's job to find talent. When you are called in by a casting director, he believes you are talent. You must show that you can display that talent. If you are talented and do not show it to the casting director, then you have no complaints about not working. If you show the talent to the casting director and the director and the producer at the audition and then find that the demands on the set are not what you expected and you cannot handle them, do not complain. On the other hand, if you have applied the technique and still have not worked, but you have had auditions, do not be discouraged. The casting directors will be trying to find a part for you. When you are called for at the auditions it means that they see the talent in you. They see that you have the tools and know how to handle them. It is their job to find the right actor for the right part, and they have you in mind. It shows that they have confidence in you.

The general interviews are very important to you. I wish that I could give you an ironclad set of rules that you could follow and ensure success. I have none. But it is my personal belief that the casting directors are all looking to be in on the discovery of the next star. It makes them look good in the eyes of the industry. Based on that belief, I think that individuality is the most important factor in the first meeting with a casting director. I do not mean you should shock him or frighten him so that he will remember you. No, I mean *you*. He thinks of you as an individual and as an actor, a film actor, and a professional one. This is about all I can think of. When you are relaxed, you show to the people you are with that you have interests, opinions, humor, considerations, etc. These are the labels you will have to display on the set, so if you have them, then you will be able to better display them. If this is a set of rules, then so be it, because that is all I believe is what the casting director looks at when you are at the general interview.

After the general interview you should call your agent and discuss with him how the interview went. You give him your impressions of the casting director's feeling about you. Tell the agent what the casting director said about the types of roles that he may place you in and about the different remarks made about your résumé and experience. This is an important part of the general interview, because it gives your agent a handle on what the casting director thinks of you in terms of roles. From there the agent then picks it up and stays with that casting director until you have started working. Once you have begun to work for that casting director, your agent has less difficulty in getting you in on auditions with him. Be accurate in your appraisal of the interview. It is to your advantage.

Your agent will usually follow up with the casting director on the auditions that you have. He will talk to that casting director about your reading and try to get an idea of how the producer and director felt about you. Most, if not all, of the agents I know do this. It is an important part in the selling of their client. It is this feedback that the agents use to make up the lists that are presented to the casting directors. Naturally, when the agent has a client who is thought of in high terms by the producers and directors, he sends that client into auditions a lot more often. On the breakdown sheets that the agent receives, the names of the producer and director and the production company are included. When you have impressed someone whose name appears on one of those breakdowns, you can bet your boots your agent is going to let the casting director know about how those people feel about you. Sometimes the casting director may forget, or there may be a different casting director on the production. It is these things that come up that your agent must contend with, and to better deal with the situation he has to have as much information as he can get. It is also a way to better understand whom in his stable of clients he should keep and whom he should let go.

The agent is in business, and if his clients do not work, he does not receive any commission—no commission, no income; no income, no business. He must remain competitive.

If the clients he has in his stable are not working, he has to find out why. He does that through the feedback he gets from the casting director.

The commercial agents are just as professional in their field. They call the casting directors of the commercials after the auditions and ask about how their clients did on the audition. If the talent does not do well on one or two auditions, the agent will not panic and let him go. But if there is a constant feedback of bad reports over a year's period, chances are the agent will cut that client loose.

This is the procedure that occurs which allows new talent in Hollywood to get an agent. It is through these openings that happen in an agents file that the new talent fill. If there is a particular type that Hollywood is looking for and the agent has one or two in his stable, but they are not winning auditions, then the agent will take on new talent and let the others go.

If a talent is let go by an agent, it does not mean that the talent is through in Hollywood. By no means. Sometimes the chemistry between agent and talent just does not seem to work. The result is that no jobs are won. It could be that an agent is pushing one particular client and not really following up on the others. Naturally those who are not being followed up on are going to suffer. If this happens, the clients who are dissatisfied look for another agent. During the switching of agents you newcomers can sneak in there.

You will give a bad reading now and then. You will feel like the whole world just fell down over your ears. And you will realize all these things after the audition. You will say to yourself, "I should have read this way" or "I should have added a little bit of business." You may hit a period where you just cannot seem to win an audition. We all go through these periods. If your agent is a professional and worth his salt, he understands that. So do not worry about it. But take a look at what you are doing at the auditions and interviews. Also, have a talk with your agent once in awhile. If you have hit one of these slow periods and you cannot seem to find the right combination to click, talk to the agent about it. Ask your agent for the feedback from the casting directors. In my personal experience I have done this. The theatrical jobs were happening for me. But the commercials had fallen off—nothing. I went to my commercial agent and had a long talk about it. She went to the casting directors and had talks with them. When it was all sorted out, what was happening was that I was not broad enough. My energy level was low. The last thing that I had expected was what was wrong! I related this story only to illustrate how the feedback from casting director to the agent can be used to your benefit. As the labels and sensory and economic levels are tools of your craft, the knowledge of the functions of the different people in the industry are the tools of the business. Use them as tools.

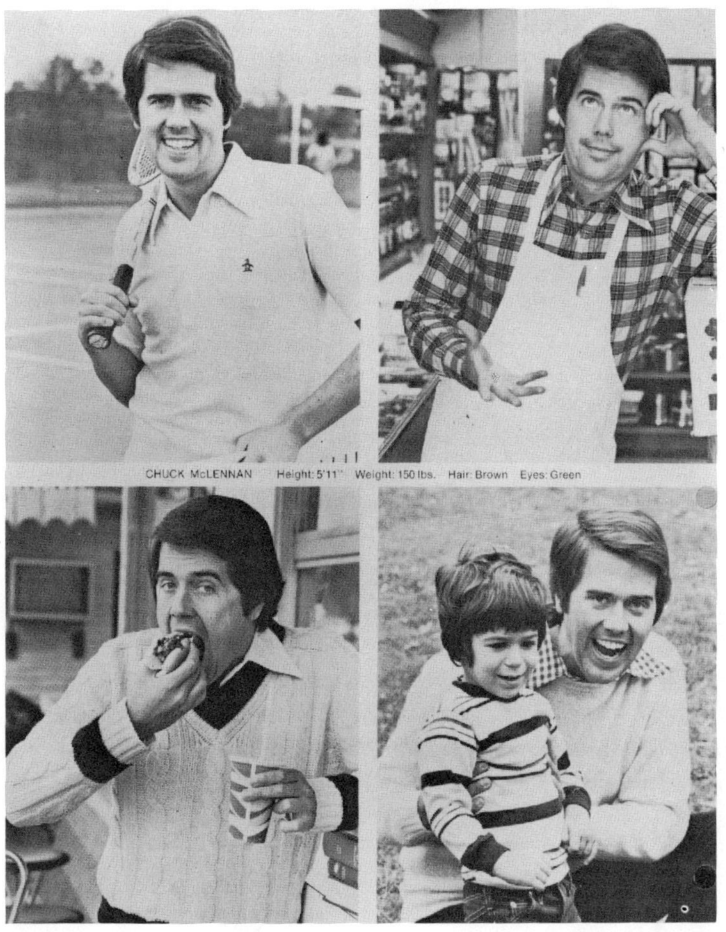

This is an example of a commercial composite. Note the variety of wardrobe of the talent. Note also that there is no resume, but there is a physical description included. Courtesy of Chuck McLennan.

JOHN LISBON WOOD

Agents: Los Angeles   New York   Hair: Brown
         BOB THORSON (213) 931-3486   JERRY KAHN (212) 582-1280   Eyes: Green

TV: Hawaii 5-O---Heads, You're Dead (Bama)---Bruce Billison

       Blue Knight---Snitch's Karma (Tonto)---Leo Penn

       Joe Forrester---Best Laid Schemes (J.D.)---Ron Kelljan

       Kojak---Sweeter than Life (Donny Collins)---Russell Mayberry

       Bronk---Cops (Al)---Don Weis

       S.W.A.T.---Counterpoint (Joey)---George McCowans

       S.W.A.T.---Helping Hand (Jamie)---Bruce Billson

Film:

       How the West was Won---Eipsode #1 (Willy)---Burt Kennedy

       Report to the Commissioner---(McDonald)---Milton Katasalas

Stage:

       The Egg---Emile Magis---Merle Oberon Theatre (A.N.T.A.) Los Angeles

       One Flew Over the Cukoo's Nest---Martini---Huntington-Hartford Theatre, L.A.

       When You Com'in Back, Red Rider?---Red Rider---East Side Play House, New York

       Hot 1 Baltimore--Jamie--Repertory, Loretto-Hilton Performing Arts Cntr., St. L.

       Detective Story---Lewis--Repertory, Loretto Hilton Performing Arts Cntr, St. L.

       Henry V---4 parts--Repertory, Loretto-Hilton Performing Arts Center, St. Louis

       Imaginary Invalid---Dr. Thomas Diafoairous--Repertory, Loretto Hilton Performing
                              Arts Center, St. Louis

This is an example of a theatrical resume. It is usually printed on the back of the actor's photo. It lists the name of the series or film, the title of the episode, the character played, and the director of the film. Courtesy of John Lisbon Wood.

THEATRICAL MOTION PICTURE
ARTISTS' MANAGER CONTRACT
(AGENCY CONTRACT)

THIS AGREEMENT, made and entered into at..., by and between

...., an artists' manager, hereinafter called the "Agent", and
(please type or print)

...., hereinafter called the "Actor",
(please type or print)

WITNESSETH :

(1) The Actor employs the Agent as his agent in theatrical motion pictures as defined in the Regulations, Amended Rule 16(f), and the Agent accepts such employment. This contract is limited to theatrical motion pictures and to contracts of the Actor as an actor in such pictures, and any reference herein to contracts or employment whereby the Actor renders his services refer to contracts or employment in theatrical motion pictures unless otherwise specifically stated.

(2) The term of this contract shall be for a period of ...., commencing ...., 19......

(3) (a) The Actor agrees to pay to the Agent as commissions a sum equal to........*10*................per cent of all moneys or other consideration received by the Actor, directly or indirectly, under contracts of employment (or in connection with his employment under said employment contracts) entered into during the term specified in Paragraph (2) or in existence when this agency contract is entered into except to such extent as the Actor may be obligated to pay commissions on such existing employment contract to another agent. Commissions shall be payable when and as such moneys or other consideration are received by the Actor, or by anyone else for or on the Actor's behalf.

(b) No commissions shall be payable on any of the following:

(i) Separate amounts paid to Actor not as compensation but for travel or living expenses incurred by Actor;

(ii) Separate amounts paid to Actor not as compensation but as reimbursement for necessary expenditures actually incurred by Actor in connection with Actor's employment, such as for damage to or loss of wardrobe, special hairdress, etc.;

(iii) Amounts paid to Actor as penalties for violations by Producer of any of the provisions of the SAG collective bargaining contracts, such as meal period violations, rest period violations, penalties or interest on delinquent payments;

(iv) Sums payable to Actors for the release on free television of theatrical motion pictures produced after January 31, 1960, under the provisions of the applicable collective bargaining agreement providing for such payment; however, if an Actor's individual theatrical motion picture employment contract provides for compensation in the event motion pictures made for theatrical exhibition are exhibited over free television, in excess of the minimum compensation payable under the Basic Contract in effect at the time the employment contract was executed, commissions shall be payable on such compensation.

(c) Any moneys or other consideration received by the Actor, or by anyone for or on his behalf, in

—1—

CM-1—THEATRICAL—1968

Example of a page from a theatrical agent contract.

SCREEN ACTORS GUILD

RIDER AUTHORIZING ONLY TELEVISION COMMERCIAL REPRESENTATION

(to be attached to TV Artists' Manager (Agency) Contract)

(A) Notwithstanding anything provided in the SAG Television Motion Picture Artists' Manager (Agency) Contract (Exhibit G), Agent is authorized to represent Actor ONLY for television commercials within the jurisdiction of Screen Actors Guild.

(B) It is expressly understood and agreed that the Agent's right to commissions on minimum reuse payments for television commercials is conditioned on faithful performance by Agent of the duties and services listed herein.

Agent shall:

(1) Seek and arrange interviews; negotiate terms and conditions of employment, and examine proposed employment contracts to check conformity with deal negotiated;

(2) Advise Actor concerning any provisions of the employment contract pertaining to exclusivity, releases, warranties or other special clauses;

(3) Maintain records and keep Actor advised of any exclusivity commitments; use best efforts to clear conflicting exclusivity commitments and engagements and obtain releases for Actor where necessary; negotiate for releases of exclusivity commitments and other restrictions where commercials have been withdrawn from use;

(4) Maintain adequate records showing dates of employment, dates of first usage, class of usage, cycles of usage, and payments made for employment and usage;

(5) Where necessary, send reminder to employer of payments due for employment and usage and promptly report to SAG any cases of repeated late payments or other violations;

(6) Where employer seeks to acquire other rights or services in addition to the performance of the Actor in the commercial, Agent shall bargain separately for such rights and services;

(7) Maintain records regarding maximum periods of use and reuse; advise Actor of expiration dates of periods of use; give written notices to advertising agencies of Actor's election not to grant right of renewed use;

(8) Make periodic inquiries to determine if commercials have been withdrawn from use;

(9) With respect to compensation for Television Commercials collected by the Agent and paid over to the Actor, the Agent shall accompany each such check with a voucher which shall contain the name of the employer or Advertising Agency, name of product, nature of payment (whether session fee, holding fee, use payment, wardrobe fee, overtime, travel time, travel expense, etc.), cycle dates and date of payment. If the voucher supplied by the Advertising Agency contains all of the information set forth above, the Agent may deliver such voucher, or a copy thereof, in lieu of a separate voucher. If the Advertising Agency or film company fails to provide the Agent with a voucher after demand therefor by the Agent, the Agent shall notify SAG to this effect but shall not be responsible for failure of the Advertising Agency or film company to deliver such voucher.

The Agent shall notify the Actor and SAG whenever a late payment penalty is due an Actor.

(C) If, during any period of 91 days immediately preceding the giving of notice of termination, the Actor fails to receive compensation in the sum of $1,500 or more for services and reuse fees for Commercials in which

TV COMMERCIALS ONLY 1968

Example of a page from a commercial agent contract.

8

Locations of Studios and Production Houses and Related Information

When the newcomer arrives in Hollywood he has a dazzling number of questions in his mind. I have covered some of them. All of them I do not think I could even guess at. But your questions concerning the business I think I can help you with. The answers to the questions I think are necessary for the business are going to be covered in this chapter. The subject here is Hollywood. Before I start, I think you should understand that the film industry is nationwide, not just Hollywood. You can work in films in many parts of the country. Television of course, is especially included. You do not have to go to Hollywood to work in films. Chicago, New York, St. Louis, Dallas, and Miami are just a few places where films are being shot every day. There are many more, and I do not want to take too much paper to name them. I am certain that there are production houses located in every state in the union, though I have no way to substantiate this.

Those of you who are presently working in the business, whether it be stage or film, I am certain have thought about making the jump to Hollywood. If you have been working stage, I hope I have brought some things to your attention about the film industry. Those of you who have been doing films like industrials and religious and educational plus the commercials and even print work (modeling): You are close to the demands you will face in the business. But, again, I hope I have shown to you the specifics that occur. I had worked the Midwest for years in films and commercials. It was not until I came to Hollywood that I realized the difference between the demands, in the productions. Not that the people in the industry outside of Hollywood are not talented. No not at all. Hollywood draws on the people from these areas. No, it is not that. The people outside of Hollywood do not think in terms of film acting. They think in terms of acting—acting as you would on the stage, taking time to do what Hollywood will demand be done instantly.

To those of you who are contemplating entering into the film career much as you would in Hollywood, you seek out an agent; get your pictures taken and printed; join a workshop; go to auditions. Your agent outside of Hollywood would see to it that you know where the studios and the producers are located. It is usually that way outside of Hollywood because the business is not very big outside of Hollywood.

There are other differences in the business outside of Hollywood also. Take the agents for example. In Hollywood you can have only one theatrical agent and one commercial agent. To have more than that would cause problems for you that you may never overcome. If you landed a job in Hollywood and you had two agents representing you, they would both be negotiating with the studio—never. The studio would not tolerate it. To say nothing of the agents. So the agents in Hollywood sign you to a contract to exclusive representation. The contract excludes commercial representation in the theatrical and vice versa for commercial. Now in Chicago I know for a fact that you can be multilisted, that is to say, you can be listed with as many agents as you wish. You can, if you choose, go exclusive. But it is not frowned upon if you do not. That is the biggest difference. Another is that there are no casting directors. So there is no casting director to contend with in your business approach. Your agent sets up the auditions directly with the director and the producer. Your agent would have to discuss your audition with the director or producer to get any feedback for you. So here your approach is different. That is in Chicago. I have heard that it is the same in New York, and I imagine that it is the same around the country.

In Hollywood you do not meet with producers except at auditions. The system is very rigid in that respect. The casting director is your only means of introduction to them within the business. You will, of course, meet the director on the set. But there the socializing is kept at a minimum. But your performance will speak for itself. And perhaps at lunch breaks you will meet people and talk. So in Hollywood you cannot expect to call on producers and directors directly. This applies to the commercial industry as well as to the theatrical.

Other areas of the country have a different pattern, especially in the commercial business. There you are encouraged to go on your own and meet the producers of the commercials at their offices. The offices are located in the different advertising agencies within that city you are in, or you can expand to the entire state. After you get the list you must find the names of the producers and the creative directors of that agency. These are the titles of the people who create and produce the commercials you see on television. Your business calls to these people should be put on the same level as the general interview in Hollywood. Your attitude would be professional, and you retain your individuality.

Also, outside of Hollywood, you can make calls on production houses. At these places you seek out the directors who are on staff. The production house may have a staff producer. If they do, you try to get an interview with him. Wherever you are located, you can begin by looking these places up in the local phone book. If you are already registered with an agent, then you should seek out the information through him. The agent will have a list of the people in town who use actors on their productions. Sometimes the agent will make a few appointments for you. But usually it is up to the individual talent to promote his or her own business. Not that the agent is unnecessary. But what these calls represent is the equivalent of the general interview in Hollywood. The agent will try to sell your talent directly to these producers and directors, and if you are a known personality, it makes the agent's job that much easier. And it brings in a lot more work for you.

This pattern is far from what happens in Hollywood. I brought it out only to show the difference in the business approach between Hollywood and the rest of the country for the actor. In Hollywood your agent is the direct contact between you and the film business. You cannot depend on a winning personality exclusively. You do not have time enough with the producers and directors. You must have control of the tools of the craft in Hollywood especially, because your meetings with the people are restricted to the interviews and auditions. If you get to know those people on a personal level you would have time to convince them of your talent and the ability to perform it in front of a camera. Outside Hollywood you can do this by repeated calls on the producers and directors. Not so in tinsel town.

To become a working film actor in Hollywood you must be a member of the Screen Actors Guild. Stage actors are members of Equity. This does not give them the right to work in film. It does allow them to join at a reduced initiation fee. But that is all. They must become members. There is another union you must sign with. That is the American Federation of Television and Radio Actors (A.F.T.R.A.).

The Screen Actors Guild covers all productions that are made on film, whether they are made in Hollywood or not. If you do a religious film or a filmed commercial or a major feature film, it is covered by this union. And you must be a member. There are productions that are nonunion. But these productions do not pay into the pension and welfare, they do not contribute toward your hospitalization. And most of all, they usually pay below scale in salary. If you choose to do these, that is up to you. I do not recommend it. If a production company needs special consideration on a film it is doing, then they contact the Guild. If the production is legitimate, then the Guild will usually go along with them. And you can, if you are a member find out from the Guild just where this production stands with the union. When you join the union, you join not only to become a professional actor, but because the union provides a great deal of protection for the actor as well as many benefits. The union sanctions seminars and helps producer's films that are designed to help the actor advance his or her career. It is a great benefit to all of us.

A.F.T.R.A. is the union that covers the television taped programs and commercials. It also covers the announcers and voice-over people in the industry. This union also provides a great deal for the actor. The benefits parallel the S.A.G. benefits. It also has a good credit union.

It is wise to join both of these unions in Hollywood. You will be issued a membership card from each of the unions. This card you will carry with you at all times. At some auditions and productions you may be asked to show your card. Better have it with you. You should be in both of the unions because of the number of shows that are taped as well as filmed. This includes the commercial industry and the industrial films. A great number of industrial films are utilizing the television tapes. There seems to be a trend toward the increased use of tapes in all of the industry.

The initiation fees and other information concerning the requirements of the unions can be obtained by writing directly to them. There are offices scattered around the country. They are listed just as I have named them here. I will give you the addresses of the two unions' offices in Hollywood:
The Screen Actors Guild Offices are located in:

Hollywood	*Florida*
7750 Sunset Blvd	3226 Ponce De Leon Blvd.
Hollywood, CA 90046	Coral Gables, FLA 33124
(213) 876-3030	(305) 444-7677

Boston
11 Beacon St. Rm 1103
Boston, Mass 02108
(617) RI2-0208

New York
551 Fifth Avenue
New York, NY 10017
(212) Murray Hill 7-4623

Chicago
307 N. Michigan Avenue
Chicago, Ill. 60601
(312) FR2-8081

San Francisco
100 Bush Street
San Francisco, CA 94104
(415) 545-3150

Detroit
28690 Southfield Road
Lathrop Village, MI 48076
(313) 559-9540

Philadelphia
1405 Locust St. Rm. 811
Philadelphia, PA 19102
(215) 545-3150

Dallas
3220 Lemmon Ave. Ste 102
Dallas, Texas 75204
(214) 522-2080

San Diego
3045 Rosecrans Bl. Rm. 206
San Diego, CA 92110
(714) 222-3996

The A.F.T.R.A. officers are sometimes located with the S.A.G. offices. If you have questions pertaining to the taped shows and joining the union, you can get the information at a S.A.G. office. However, for your information, the national A.F.T.R.A. office is located at:

American Federation of Television & Radio Artists
1350 Avenue of the Americas
New York, NY 10019

The Hollywood office is located at:

American Federation of Television Radio & Artists
1717 North Highland Avenue
Hollywood, CA 90028
(213) 461-8111

S.A.G. offers many seminars and information to the new-comer in Hollywood. One of the problems that new actors have is the lack of film on themselves. Many times a producer or director will ask for film. Unfortunately, Hollywood film is what they consider important enough to look at. Through S.A.G. you may be able to get some. They work in conjunction with the A.F.I. These are the initials for the American

Film Institute. This organization trains and educates people in the other disciplines of the film industry. S.A.G. will submit your picture to them for the films that they make with their students. These are student workshop films, but many of them are very well done. And they are done according to the standards of the film industry. Also throughout the year A.F.I., along with S.A.G. casting directors, successful actors, and directors, will give talks on the film industry. So you can see the union can be very helpful in many ways.

When you arrive in Hollywood, your choice of location for your home should be made with the location of the studios in mind. California has an excellent freeway system, and getting to the studios really presents no problems. But if you live far away, the auditions can be a problem. When you have an audition at 10 A.M. at one studio and another at 3 P.M. at a studio close by, you will have to find a way to spend the time between auditions. If you live too far from Hollywood, then you cannot spend the time at home. You have to find another way to spend the time, which can be difficult.

The overwhelming majority of the commercial production houses are located in Hollywood. I will not include the addresses of these because there are so many of them. And your commercial agent will give you the specific address when you go for the auditions. So it actually is enough to know that Hollywood is the location of the commercial production houses.

Of the major film studios only two are located a long distance from the other large studios. These are Metro-Goldwyn-Mayer and Twentieth-Century Fox. They are large studios and very active studios, and you will undoubtedly visit them in your career.

M-G-M is located in Culver City. Culver City is a western suburb of Los Angeles. From central Hollywood it is a good thirty-five-minute drive through the city. Twentieth-Century is located north of M-G-M, but just as far west. Twentieth is located in west Los Angeles, and the drive from Hollywood to Twentieth is about the same in time.

The rest of the major studios and networks are in a rather small radius of central Hollywood. The list of them is not in any particular order, except for the geographical location. The valley refers to the San Fernando Valley, which is just over the hill from Hollywood to the north.

Several of the television networks have two locations, such as A.B.C. and C.B.S. There are studios in both of these locations. You will find yourself rehearsing in one and shooting the actual taping in another. Of the local television stations that I have listed you may wonder a bit. Business has been so good here in Hollywood for the independents that studio space is at a premium, and the local stations that have taken over some of the old film studios are now renting stage space for the different taped shows. The case of Channel 5 KTLA is a fine example. That station is the original Warner Bros. Studio. Many a classic movie was shot there. When Warner Bros. expanded their operation they sold the location in the 1930s and moved to Burbank. So much for incidental bits of information. But you can see that KTLA is capable of supplying stage space for television shows.

These are the locations:

Burbank Studios
(Warner Bros.)
4000 Warner Bld.
Burbank, Ca.

C.B.S. Studios
7800 W. Beverly Blvd.
Los Angeles, Ca.

C.B.S. Studios
4024 Radford
Studio City, Ca.

Columbia Studios
300 Colgems Sq.
Burbank, Ca.

Columbia Ranch
3701 W. Oak
Burbank, Ca.

Culver City Studios
9336 W. Washington
Culver City, Ca.

Disney Studios
500 Buena Vista
Burbank, Ca.

General Services Studios
1040 N. Las Palmas
Hollywood, Ca.

Goldwyn Studios
1041 N. Formosa
Hollywood, Ca.

K.A.B.C. (Ch. 7 Network)
Prospect & Talmadge
Hollywood, Ca.

K.A.B.C. (Ch. 7 Network)
1313 N. Vine
Hollywood, Ca.

Metro Goldwyn Mayer Studios
10202 W. Washington Blvd.
Culver City, Ca.

K.T.L.A. (Ch. 5 Indept.)
5800 Sunset Blvd.
Hollywood, Ca.

Paramount Studios
5441 W. Marathon
Hollywood, Ca.

K.N.B.C. (Ch. 4 Network)
3000 Alameda
Burbank, Ca.

Twentieth Century Fox Studios
10201 W. Pico Blvd.
Los Angeles, Ca.

K.T.T.V. (Ch. 11 Indpt.)
5746 Sunset Blvd.
Hollywood, Ca.

Universal Studios
100 Universal City Plaza
Universal City, Ca.

The studios located in the valley are easily reached by taking the Hollywood Freeway over the Cahuenga Pass or Laurel Canyon Road over the mountain.

Using the location of the A.F.T.R.A. office as a central location, that is 1717 N. Highland Avenue, you would be at Hollywood Boulevard in Hollywood. From that location to the Burbank Studios it would take you about fifteen minutes under normal driving conditions. The Burbank Studios are located at the eastern end of the valley. From the Burbank Studio to the Columbia Studio is a five-minute walk. The Columbia lot is at the eastern end of the Burbank Studio lot. You can enter through Burbank and walk through the lot to Columbia or vice versa. They each have their own gates, but the lots are connected.

From the Burbank Studio NBC and Disney Studios are a little north and east. Driving time would be five minutes to NBC and ten minutes to Disney.

West from Burbank Studio, Universal is less than five minutes. CBS is another ten minutes west.

You can see that even if your auditions are in the valley you do not have far to go from one studio to another.

In Hollywood, Paramount and Goldwyn Studios are only a short distance from each other. From Highland and Hollywood Boulevards to MGM or Twentieth would be the longest drive to get to. There, as I said, it would take about thirty-five to forty minutes under normal traffic conditions.

The independent producers may have offices at locations other than the studios, but those you would have to get from the agent as you get your auditions.

9

An Average Workday on the Set and on Tape Shows

The first interview with the first audition and the first job—they are all unsettling. A person who is normally very calm will find himself sweating and uncertain, fighting to control his hands and his voice. We have all experienced it. So if you do, do not feel as though you are the only one who ever has. It comes from not knowing what to expect, from wondering if you can do the job you were called in for. Everything around you will be strange. The officer, the people, the secretaries, the reception clerks—all will have a look of total indifference toward you. They display no interest in you at all. This, coupled with not knowing what to expect, is what makes you nervous. As an actor you have a certain amount of nervous energy that you will always experience. This is a part of the business. You will learn to control that as you progress through the film industry. But when you are new at something, everything is magnified. Now, by new, I mean new in Hollywood. The things that are magnified are always the negative aspects. When you walk into the office of some studio casting director, the receptionist asks your name in a tone that you take as impolite. When you are new, that is what it seems like. It may be that she is busy, but at this time it does not occur to you. No, she is just impolite. When you talk to someone, or ask him a question, he seems to resent you bothering them. Well, do not take it that way, because it will probably not be so. When that happens, it happens because you are unfamiliar with the surroundings and the people. You could not know what the procedure is if you have never been through it or had it explained to you. That is what I am going to cover here. I am covering this in detail so that you are acquainted, if not familiar, with how the entire procedure unfolds from the audition to the job. When you have some knowledge of what is going to happen on that first audition, it will help to calm you down. Maybe with a good start you can go all the way. A bad start may slow you down quite a bit.

The uncertainty about what happens, or is expected of you, can have an effect on your attitude. We know that the wrong attitude can affect your audition or interview. Also, you can put your attention on what you are there for: the audition or the interview.

Experienced actors many times find themselves in the same difficulty as the beginning actors, but for a different reason. The businesslike attitude of the people involved in the film industry, from file clerks to executive producers, is mistaken for indifference. To some actors walking in for an audition and being treated with indifference by everybody from the moment they get there is intolerable. After enjoying some degree of popularity from wherever they came from, they find it difficult to be unrecognized as an actor. They fail to accept the fact that the people in the film industry in Hollywood deal with actors all day long, every day, from day players to superstars. To them the business is important, they do their business without being unduly impressed. The actor, on the other hand, feels that the recognition that he or she received in the past is due now in the present. A feeling such as this can set off a bad attitude in the experienced actor just as the unfamiliarity can do to the inexperienced one. If the experienced actor allows himself to be aggravated in this way, it is unfortunate, because it has to have an effect on the audition.

Other actors go to extremes to get the casting director and the office people to remember them. One actor I know of sat in on his general interview and constantly burped, while he gave a long dissertation on how much he knew and how little Hollywood knew. At another general interview he stuck his tongue out at the casting director, not once but several times. He did all these things with the best of intentions for his own career. But, unfortunately, the casting directors did not see it that way. They called his agent and made some very specific remarks about how they felt regarding this type of performance and felt that they should not have their valuable time spent in this fashion. I am certain that the casting director will remember this particular performer for sometime. But the question is, how will he remember him? The sad thing about this little story is that he is a very accomplished actor with many impressive stage credits. I wonder what he is doing now. Maybe he went back to where he received those impressive credits.

His intention, of course, was to impress the casting directors, and consequently they would remember him. He showed them that he was uninhibited, and so relaxed that he did not give a damn. Well he did just that. Unfortunately the casting directors are looking for professionals who do give a damn. Also, they did remember him, long enough to call his agent and tell him about the interview.

Maybe it was nerves. Maybe it was overreacting to the indifference of everybody at the studio. Whatever caused him to do that backfired on him. So you have to be careful not to let those things get to you. If you do, maybe you will overreact.

The series of events that occur before your first job begin after the agent has submitted your picture for a particular role in a particular show. The casting director will call your agent and give him an audition time and location. This information the agent then relates to you. And you are on your way.

When you get to the studio, you ask for the casting office. You go to that. There will be a receptionist busy behind a desk. The room will probably be a little crowded. Give the receptionist your name. She will look it up on a casting sheet. The sheet contains the role you are reading for and the scenes you are to read. The names of the other actors auditioning for the same part are on there also. After she has found your name and checked it off, she will hand you a few pages from the script of the show. Sometimes you will get the entire script. The number of actors auditioning for the same part varies. Do not let that concern you. The receptionist marks your arrival time down alongside your name. You are called in for your reading in the order of your arrival.

When your name is called, the casting director will lead you to the office of the producer. When you walk in, the casting director will introduce you to the people in the room. The director or producer or both will definitely be there. They will talk a bit and then ask if you have looked at the script and are ready to read.

After your reading the casting director will walk out with you. Remain pleasant and do not ask how you did. You will find that out later.

You will get a phone call from your agent telling you that you have won the job. That is your first contact about work. He will tell you the day or days that you are booked, what role you are to play, and the rate you receive for your performance. After you have this information you must immediately notify your commercial agent. You tell the commercial agent the exact information that you have, the days you are to work, the role you are to play, and the show you are on. Your commercial agent will then put those days aside and will not book you for commercials or auditions. The information about the role you are to play and the show that you are on your commercial agent will use as credits for you to commercial producers and casting people. If the situation were reversed and your commercial agent booked you then you would immediately notify your theatrical agent. Do not fail to notify the agents. It is very important. Any double bookings can cause a real upheaval. Besides, the theatrical agent will use your commercial credits to his casting people.

Now that you have been notified of your "call" day, you will next receive your script. Most of the time it is delivered to you by messenger. If it is not delivered, then your agent will tell you where to pick it up. Most likely it will be at the office where you auditioned. The next phone call you get will be from the wardrobe department. For some reason that usually comes around 6 P.M. Do not ask me why, because I do not know; it just does. When you receive the call they will ask you for your size of shoes, hat, gloves, and whatever else you will be wearing on the show. After that has been established, the wardrobe department will give you a date and time for a fitting. You will get paid for the fitting day. If they ask you when it is convenient for you, make it convenient so that you are there on time. If they do not ask you and just tell you what time and where to be, then you be there on time anyway.

If you are to report on the lot for the fitting, then the wardrobe department will make the arrangements for you to have a pass to get in. The pass will be at the gate. All you have to do is give the guard your name and tell him where you are going. On the pass there is a parking space number. The number will correspond to the number on the parking spaces. This is your reserved space; use it. Do not park in somebody else's spot. You may not know whose it is.

Do not hesitate to ask the guard where the wardrobe department is. Some of the lots are quite large. You can depend on the guard to give you the right directions. Somebody else may just be a visitor, or new like yourself.

At the wardrobe department you look for the sign with the name of the show you are working. If you cannot find that, then ask for the person who called you. After your fitting it is not necessary for you to sign anything to prove that you were there so that you can get paid. It is an automatic process.

The next call you get concerning the show will be your agent again. But this time it will be your work call. You will be told the stage number you are to report to, and you will be given two times. The first one is for makeup, the second is on set. So your call would be something like this: 7:30 makeup, 8:00 on set, stage 32. That time for on the set means that you are on the set and ready to work. Not rehearse or discuss, but to work.

When you drive up to the studio your pass will be at the gate. Park your car and walk to the stage. You do not have to worry about wardrobe. It will be there. When you get to the stage, report to the assistant director. Once you have reported to the A.D. he will introduce you to the makeup person, who will probably be on the stage. The A.D. will show you to your dressing room. Wardrobe will place your wardrobe in your dressing room. Your name will be on the dressing room door so as to avoid mistakes. After makeup you go back to your dressing room and get into your wardrobe. That completed, go back to the stage and to the A.D. The A.D. will have a call sheet with him. The call sheet will show the scenes that are to be shot on that stage. If you have more than one scene on that stage he can tell you which will shoot first. If you have scenes on other locations, the A.D. can tell you what sequence they will be shot in. Your main contact on the set is the A.D. If there is time before your scene is to be shot, you can go back to your dressing room if you choose. But you must report that to the A.D. He has to know where you are at all times, even if you go to the "john." If you decide to stay and watch the shooting, there are chairs provided for the cast. The chairs marked with a name are for those people only, so do not use them. These chairs are there because the producers want you to be fresh when you start the scene. Many people not in the industry think that those chairs are there because the actors are temperamental. Not so. They are there because the producers are all business. They hired you, and they want you fresh when you work. Much of the time you spend on the set is waiting for the scene to be set up, (the camera angles, the lighting, etc.). If you had to just stand around while the crew is setting up the scene, your face would show fatigue. On your close-ups that would be terrible, especially if your character is not supposed to be fatigued.

The Assistant Director will have some papers for you to sign. These are your contracts. You keep one copy and the production company keeps the rest. Your rate will be typed in on the contract, as well as the role you are playing. The A.D. (Assistant Director) will also have your W 2's for you to fill out. If you are working as a day player and your rate is $300, and you are working two days, then the government will take out taxes appropriate to that amount. However, the amount of tax should not be as high as will be taken because of the working conditions. That is that you may not work again the rest of the week or even the rest of the month. So one of the papers you will want to have there is a "Declaration Regarding Income Tax Withholding." Some production companies provide these declarations, others do not. So it will behoove you to have them with you when you report to work. The taxes on a daily basis are very large. You can substantially reduce that by filling out one of these declarations.

If you are to do a location job, the studio will provide transportation for you. If they do not and you provide your own transportation, then the A.D. will pay you in cash at the end of the shooting. The amount is paid according to the number of miles to location from the studio. If the transportation is provided, then you would report to the studio the same as you do for a job on the lot. You would report to the A.D. He will assign you to a car for the trip. You will ride with the other actors on the film. Do not get confused with the bus that the extras ride in and the vehicle that the actors ride in. An actor here in California on his first show did that. The confusion that happened is in a way funny, but also, in a way, not so funny.

He was working at Twentieth-Century Fox on a major television show. The film was shooting on location. He reported to someone who was not the A.D. This person (whoever he was) acknowledged his arrival. After a short time everyone who was just standing around started to get on the buses when they were told to. Our friend joined them. The bus took them to the location, which was over an hour's drive. When they arrived there was the usual hustle and bustle of setting the shot up. Our friend just stood around waiting for someone to tell him what to do. Meanwhile the director has asked the assistant director to get the actor for the scene. The assistant director did not remember putting our friend into a car, and he asked the other actors if any of them had ridden with our friend. They, of course, said no. Well, all Hell broke loose. The A.D. thought that he had left our friend at the studio. He immediately sent a car back to the studio to get him. All through this chaos our friend was standing among the extras waiting for someone to tell him what to do. First, our friend did not realize that the people he was with were extras. He thought they were actors as he was. Second, he did not know what all the excitement was about. Finally, he let his curiosity get the better of him and went and asked someone what was happening. The someone he asked was the Director! It was then explained to him, in firm terms, that the actors do not ride with the extras.

It all worked out all right. But still it was embarrassing to my friend. And the A.D. was made to look bad in the eyes of the production company. Try to avoid those situations. You should be able to now that you know who to see, and what happens when reporting to your first job.

After you have worked a few shows it will become old hat to you. The people on the crew will begin to know you, the

A.D.'s will be familiar with you, and you can be a lot more relaxed on the set. Those first shows are the rough ones. Now that you are informed, some of the roughness is smoothed down a bit.

When you are working on a hot set your job is to act. If there is something to be moved or rearranged, you do not do it. There is someone working the set that the job is assigned to. Some member of the crew will have the job and in no uncertain terms will tell you to keep your hands off. The film industry is highly unionized, and they are jealous of their jobs. So if you do something on that set that a stagehand could have done, he resents it. And he will tell you so. If you are not accustomed to having things done for you, you better become accustomed, from makeup to wardrobe on down.

After you have finished the job, the A.D. will have you sign a time card. If you work more than eight hours, you are paid for it. This card is what establishes your hours. If you have worked more than eight hours, be certain the times are filled in before you sign. If you have worked more than eight hours and have not been paid for it, this card is referred to. The A.D. could make a mistake and fill in the wrong times. If he does and you claim overtime, you will not have a leg to stand on.

That just about covers the information you will need to know about working a film job. Essentially what it amounts to is getting to the right person on the set. That is the A.D. The director will talk to you about the scene you are to do. He is very busy during a shooting and he cannot be bothered with all the nickle and dime stuff that you have to go through. So when you speak with the director, talk about the film. Talk about the script, choices, labels, etc. Do not bother him with questions about anything else. Talk only business, film business.

The other type of show you will be performing in I have mentioned only once before. That is the taped show, in front of a live audience. Some shows are taped, but not in front of a live audience. I have worked a children's show like that. If that is the case for you someday, then the reporting procedures are the same as for film. You will shoot your scenes, sometimes out of context, work the number of days that you were hired for, and that is that. The live show is a completely different pattern.

The audition is, of course, the same for the taped shows as for the filmed ones. So that we can skip over. The wardrobe call will be the same as with the filmed shows. So that also can be skipped over. But your booking is different. You will be booked for more than one day—probably five days.

You will be reporting to a television station. The stages at the television stations are about as large as those on the film lots, but there are some obvious differences. The stage will have a permanent set built on it for the show. There will be a master control booth somewhere nearby, if not directly on the stage. The control booth is where the director is when you are doing camera rehearsals and shooting the show.

When you report to the stage you report to the floor director. He is the equivalent to the A.D. in films. His job is a bit more complicated, however, since he must be on the floor (the set) at all times, during rehearsal and shooting. During the camera rehearsal and the shooting, he wears a headphone and microphone and carries a script. With the script he follows the progress of the show, line for line. With the headphone he receives directions from master control and relays them to the cast and crew.

The first day you will be given a dressing room and meet the cast. On this day you sit around a table and read the script. At this point there may be some changes as the cast works out the kinks in the lines. By the end of the day you will have worked out the cues with the other actors. The director and the writers are here at this time to make suggestions.

On the second day the script should be memorized. If it is not, do not panic. Just be certain that you have the script with you for reference. There will be a script girl there following the lines. If you forget a line, then just call for the line to her. She will give it to you, and you will not have to break rhythm. By the end of this day the show will be moving along smoothly, and be ready for timing.

The third day the director will work on specific "blocking" of the show. You will run through the lines several times, and then he will time the show and begin to block it. All that blocking means is that your movements are to be in specific places on the set. And to be on specific lines. The director works this out with the actors. But the director has to keep camera movements in mind. To aid him in this area is the technical director. You, as an actor, will have very little to do with the technical director. The director of the taped show will usually have three cameras to work with. As he sits in the control room he controls the movements of the camera operated through headphones by giving directions to each cameraman. He has a television screen for each camera so that he can see what the camera sees. Through the microphone the director will tell each cameraman whether he should zoom in or out, take a two shot, or a full shot, or where to move the camera. The technical director aids him in these operations.

On the fourth day the show will have a camera rehearsal. Now the blocking is tested to see how it comes across on camera. All through the camera rehearsal you speak your lines, even though the performance is interrupted frequently. On this day the director is in the control room. The floor director is there on the set to relay the directions. He comes down only to work some scene where the blocking is not as smooth as it should be. The blocking that was worked out by the director without the camera is usually changed considerably this day. On one of the shows that I worked it took the director, the technical director, and the producer to work out the blocking to get six men out of one corner. It took these men several hours to work it out.

By the end of this day the show will be at the final timing and blocking. The show is now ready to go.

The next day, the fifth day, taping day, your call will be for rehearsal, dress rehearsal, and taping. When you first arrive you will have several run-throughs of the show. These will be with the cameras. About an hour before the dress rehearsal you will get a break. At this time the cast will go to makeup and get into wardrobe. The makeup person will be right on the set, so you do not have to go far.

Soon the first audience will begin to file in. You get the call, "Places everyone." The cameramen, the crew, and the cast all go to their places. A warmup person begins to talk to the audience. Sometimes the warmup person is a comedian, sometimes it is the director or the producer. He sets the audience into the mood by telling them of the show and introducing the stars. His job is to loosen the audience up so that they will respond to the show. After the warmup there is a pause, a call for "Quiet on the set," and action. The show begins.

The show will run its course through the dress rehearsal. The audience response is measured here. The audience numbers about three hundred. After the dress rehearsal the warmup man comes out again and introduces the rest of the cast to the audience. Then the audience files out of the stage area.

After the dress rehearsal is completed and the audience has left, all the cast members, the director, producers, writers, and the floor director return into what is called the "green room." The green room is a room set aside on the stage that has comfortable chairs and sofas, and tables much like a parlor would have. The producer will have provided a catered dinner at this time for the cast. There will be coffee and sometimes some liquor. But before the cast can sit down to eat, the director begins discussing the show. He will break down the audience reaction to the different scenes. He will talk to the actors who he feels can get more laughs from the lines they have. He will make changes in the blocking if he feels it will help the show. The writers will put their two cents in and try to improve the show for the second performance. Generally this gathering is for the improving of the show for the actual taping. This dress rehearsal was taped, and the laugh tract was recorded. But for some reason it is called a rehearsal and the second performance is called the taping.

The time for the taping will come and the second audience begins to file in. The same procedure occurs. The warmup person begins this bit, and the show will start. If during the taping an actor has blown a line, or something else occurs that should not, the director will "stop tape." If this happens to you, do not feel bad. It has happened many times to many actors. The director will say to the actor, or even to the entire cast, what he wants done. This he does over a loudspeaker system. On one show I did, one of the actors blew his lines. So the director stopped tape and called to him to try again. He did try again, and again he blew the lines. So the director stopped tape and called to him the second time. The actor tried for the third time, but this time the lines were correct but the reading was wrong. The director interrupted him in the middle of the reading and told him to start again and get it right. Well, the actor turned, looked at the control room, and said, "I will if you stop interrupting me." Well, it broke the audience up. They roared with laughter, because the way the actor said it was funny. His attitude was perfect. Many of us might have panicked and made the situation take on a serious air. After all, we do not appreciate making a mistake in front of three-hundred people and then having someone tell us about it over a loudspeaker. But that actor kept control and a good attitude and turned it into a funny situation. After he made his remark and the audience laughed the tension that was building up broke. On his next delivery the lines were correct and he was on the button. Not only that, the audience was much more responsive after that. So responsive that after the show the director came down and congratulated him on his performance to the audience. They in turn applauded him, because they enjoyed the entire episode. He had managed to make his mistake a part of the show. This is the personal touch that the audience seeks when they come to see the taping. So if it happens to you, do not panic. Treat it lightly while you are trying to correct the line. Do not be embarrassed. It is part of the job.

When the show has been completed the warmup person again brings out the cast and introduces them to the audience. When the stage has emptied the director calls the cast for pickups. He needs these now because, although the cameras are mobile, their movements are restricted by the set. Each camera is set on wheels so that the cameraman has control of where the camera is placed. He moves it with ease, but the cameras are forced to move around the props that are on the set, around the walls of the set, etc. Close-ups during the actual taping are almost impossible to get unless the actor is in a certain position. Again, the actor is in a situation where he must perform out of context of the scene.

The pickups that the director gets here will be used as a sort of exclamation point for the scene. He may use some of the pickups for the finished product or he may use all of them or none of them. There are many factors that must be considered by the director for the finished show. Time is the major one. It is the only one, I believe, that concerns us. However, there are occasions where the director asks for pickups from the cast that would be inserted into the previous week's show. This occasion happened to me. The director had decided to add a character to the show. I was that character. To establish the character, and carry the story line into the next week, he had us improvise a brief scene. That scene was added to the tape of the previous week's show. That does not happen too often, but like so many things in the film industry, it does happen!

The shows are taped in advance of the date to be shown on television. Some are taped well in advance, others are only two weeks ahead of air date. One filmed television show was finished the week of the air date!

After you have completed your pickups the floor director will release you. But you are not released until he does it. When you have finished the show, do not just wash up and leave. That is a mortal sin.

The contracts that you will sign for the taped shows are from A.F.T.R.A. They are very similar to the S.A.G. contracts. You must sign contracts for each show that you do. The only exception is when you are a regular on a show. Then you sign the contracts that have been negotiated for the season.

That just about covers what happens in the making of a taped show in Hollywood. Many unexpected things occur during rehearsal. Everybody is a little nervous and edgy. Mistakes will happen, so expect the unexpected. To handle the unexpected you have to be in control of your craft. You can be in control by using the tools. And another bit of information here, on any job you go on, tape or film, bring that script with you. When you are rehearsing the tape shows, have that script close by, even though there is a script girl on the set. When there are script changes, from lines to blocking to actions, mark them on your script for quick reference. There are many things that you will have to remember during rehearsal, just as everybody else has a lot to remember, and if you forget a line or action during rehearsal you have a quick reference. It will not be necessary to bother others on the show. During the first day's line reading you will probably make a lot of notes on it. It would be wise to mark the changes that the other actors have in the show. Any little bit of business that you can add to your part by playing off the other actors is good for the show. The information you add to your script may come in handy even though it concerns only the other actors.

We have discussed the film shows and the tape shows. That brings us to the commercials. The world of commercials, though related to the film industry, is rapidly becoming an industry in its own right. The demands are beginning to take on a different appearance than those of the rest of the industry. The other disciplines in the commercial films are becoming so specialized that it seems they do not enter the other areas. The directors of commercials are an example. Some of those with whom I have spoken have no interest in expanding into the feature films or situation shows on television. They say that commercials are so demanding that they are more satisfying when they are completed. They have no interest in moving to other areas of the film industry.

When you have people who are that dedicated to one particular phase of any industry, that part of the industry is going to have number of specialized demands. We covered what I believe are the effects of those demands on the actor. Here I will show how a typical commercial runs its course, and show the differences between them and the rest of the industry for the actor. You know how to approach the performance required of you. You had that in the exercises. You will work from that point of view. I am making this an issue here because you will be dealing with a different outlook on the part of the director and the producer as far as what they want on the finished product.

The first difference you will find is in the auditions. When you are called by your agent for a commercial audition you are given the location of the audition. It may be at a casting director's office, or the production company office, or the advertising agency office. Next you are given the time you are to be at the audition. Then you are told what product this audition is for (this is very important), and last but not least, what they are looking for as far as characterization is concerned.

I noted the importance of the product for which you are to audition. This is because you cannot have conflicting products in your running commercials. When you do a commercial for a product, you are paid because your image is there in sort of endorsement of that product. The clients of competing products will not allow you to appear for theirs. And products that you have already done commercials for will not permit you to do a competing product commercial. And they have the right to stop you. There have been cases where the actor has had a commercial running for a product, and made a commercial for a competing product. When it was discovered, the actor had to pay the entire cost of the commercial that he did. He was fortunate in that the mistake was caught before it hit the air. If it had not been, then he would have had to pay much more.

When you get to the audition you will find a larger number of people are there to audition for the job. The casting director will have a sheet set aside for the talent to sign in on./ You find that sheet. It has a space for your name, your Social Security number, the name of your agent, the time of your call, the time you arrived, the time you left, your initials, and a series of numbers. The numbers are for the times you are called back. So in this instance you would circle number one.

After you sign in, you look for the storyboard and or the script. The storyboard is a series of drawn pictures to give a visual idea of what is to occur. Below the pictures are the lines that are spoken at the time. If you do not have a storyboard, then work from the script. The casting director will take the talent into the audition from the list according to their arrival, unless she is trying to match up a family or group. In that case she already has in mind who is going to be called in with whom. This is one of the reasons that it is important to be on time. The casting director will make your audition time with your agent to correspond with the times of the other talent you are to audition with.

After you have been brought into your audition, the casting director will leave. She leaves you with the director, the agency producer, and perhaps a writer from the agency. They will talk to you about what you are doing in films and television and then ask you what you have running. This is to find out for their client if you have a conflict, and also to see if you have too many commercials running. If you do, they will consider you overexposed. They will discuss briefly what the commercial is about then ask if you have had time to look at the script, and then ask you to read.

There is another type of commercial audition at which you will frequently appear. That is the taped audition. These are conducted by the casting director. Your audition is put on tape and sent to the agency. The clients then can audition at their leisure.

Commercial auditions sometimes run over a period of days. Even weeks. They extend into what are called "callbacks." These callbacks are sort of a filtering process. The clients are so careful in producing these commercials because they represent the product on the air to the public, and also, like the rest of Hollywood, because the client spends a lot of money on them. If you get callbacks on commercials, your agent is very happy. It is almost like winning the job to them. When you report to the callbacks and sign in on the sheet, you will circle the number that corresponds to your callback. It is important, because you get paid if the callbacks exceed three, and also, if you are kept over an hour, you are paid. It is wise to be accurate on these sign in sheets.

After you have won the job, the agent is notified by the casting director. She gives your agent the time and the date of the shooting. Your agent, in turn, calls you and gives you the work call. All the notifications are the same as those in the film industry. Your wardrobe call is sometimes different. In commercials you will be told what wardrobe to bring to the production company for a wardrobe "check," and on which day. This would be the equivalent of the wardrobe call for a film. The difference, of course, is that you bring a selection of your own clothes according to what the production assistant or casting director tells you to bring.

When you arrive at the production company for the wardrobe check, the producer, director, and the production assistant make the choices for your wardrobe. If the wardrobe required was something specialized, such as a uniform or gown or tuxedo, then the wardrobe will be rented for you at one of the many costume houses in Hollywood. In this case, the fitting date would be given to you by the production assistant. She would give you the location and the time for the fitting. You would have to go to the costume house for the fitting.

Now you have won the job and gone on your wardrobe check. The next step is the job. If it is a location job and the company wants you to report on location, you will be given a map while you are at the wardrobe check. The map will also state the time and the date of the shoot. If it is a studio job, then you have to get the address for that too. Many of the commercial production houses do not maintain a studio, nor do many of them maintain much of a permanent staff. When they do a job they will rent studio space and equipment. In any case, the majority of the jobs are shot on location.

Let us assume that for this job you are on location. When you arrive, the crew will be setting up the shot. You seek out the director. That is right, the director. Let him know that you are there and ready for work. In some instances you will bring the wardrobe with you that was chosen at the wardrobe check. In others they will keep the wardrobe with them and bring it along on the shoot. But you are at the job. You have checked in with the director. Also at this time you will see that there are more people at the shoot who are not part of the cast or the crew. These are the clients. They are people from the ad agency, agency producers, copywriters, and art directors. These are some of the people that attend the shoot from the ad agency. There also may be what is called a client representative. The word *client* here refers to the client of the ad agency. He or she is a V.I.P. He usually has the final word on what you do. On some shoots they are all there. On others the art director alone may represent the whole bunch, or any combination of them may be there.

The A.D. may be the one to show you to the dressing room, which, on location will be a trailer. This choice is sometimes handled by the production assistant. But somebody will show you the dressing room. If you do not have the script, this is the time to get it. Even if you have the script, it may be wise to ask if there have been any changes. Find out from the director if you should change into wardrobe right away. The shot may take some time to set up, and you could soil your wardrobe if you sit around in it too long. The setting up of the props in the scenes for a commercial take a great deal longer than in television film. This is because the people who watch the commercials are very critical if there is the slightest mistake. I mean it. The viewer will write a letter to the sponsor if he sees something in the commercial that is not correct. The sponsor then comes down hard on the advertising agency. So they really try to make everything perfect.

When the set is correct, the lighting is perfect, and the sound is right, you are called. Now the director will spend some time with you. If it is a direct pitch to camera that you are involved in, he will time you. Now if the commercial runs for thirty seconds, your delivery should be completed in twenty-five. It would be smart of you to check on this when you first arrive, because I have been stunned many times by working my copy down to twenty-five seconds, only to find out just before we shoot that they need it in twenty seconds.

If your commercial is one of actions from you, the director will have a run-through. At this time the client is watching. You will complete your action. The director will say, "O.K. Hold that." Then he turns to the client and whispers to him. They both look at you, then they whisper to the cameraman. The director will say, "O.K. Do it again on action." They all stare. You do your action. The director says, "Cut. Hold it there." The client then looks into the eyepiece of the camera. Then the director and he whisper again. They turn and whisper to the cameraman. Then they all turn and stare at you. By this time you are beginning to wonder if you have done something wrong! You begin to doubt if you are qualified for the job. All these doubts—and you have not even performed yet!

After a while the director says, "O.K. Let's try one." "Whew," you say to yourself. "I did it right." You perform the action. The director says "Cut. Print." Wow, one in the can! Wait—the director turns and whispers to the client. The client looks at you, turns back to the director and whispers to him. Then they both turn and stare. Meanwhile you are just remaining in your final position and nobody is whispering to you. Then, "O.K. Let's try it again... but little more in it, actor." "Oh, Oh," you think, but you say "O.K. will do." The call for sound, camera, and action—you do it again. The cut. Then the same as before. They turn to each other and whisper. This goes on for maybe four or five takes. They will probably print each one, but they will keep taking them. If you do not know the business you would begin to think that maybe you should get into a different business. But when you become familiar with the industry you will realize that they are taking into consideration the lighting, the background, and a multitude of other things that can influence the overall commercial. Even with that information firmly implanted in your mind it can get to youm It has to me. But each time I ask them, "Was it O.K.?" They say, "Oh, yes. That was fine." Then they turn and start whispering again.

While the client and the director are there in conference you are on a hot set. And I mean hot. The lights are burning down on you and you can feel yourself wilt. After a few takes and a few more conferences, the director will say to you, "Ahhh, makeup. See if you can touch the actor a bit. He seems to be sweating." So makeup comes to you and says, "I'll see what I can do." Then the director says, "remember how you did the first take. Well, that was the best so far. Let's do it again. And do it the way you did it on the first take. O.K. Let's go." "Aha!" you say to yourself. "What was that?" I thought I did each one the same way." That is probably right, so do not panic. Just do it again. If there was a movement or gesture that you did and you miss it on this take, the director will tell you what it is. The important thing is not to panic. Remain in control. It will come out right, believe me. If you have your tools at your command, there is no problem for you. It sounds a great deal more frightening than it actually is. Remember, also, that the director is there to help you get it right. But he has many things to watch. Everything must be correct. It is up to him to see that it is correct. It is up to you to perform correctly, and you can.

When there is sound on the commercial, that is to say, when they are recording your lines as you perform the action, you will hear several commands from the director before he gives you your cue. There will be replies to each one. Before he wants you go to into action the director must be certain that the sound man and the cameraman are ready and rolling. So he calls, "Sound." The reply from the sound man is "Speed." Then he calls, "Camera." The reply from the cameraman is "Rolling." He then calls for a slate. This wooden device has spaces for the scene number, take number, production name, and director's name. This device has a hinged part at the top, painted with diagonal white stripes. The man who slates will call the scene and the take number. It is after this that the director calls for action. The slate is for the film editor. The vocal slate is for the soundtrack.

If the shoot is without sound or dialogue, the slate is still used to the camera. But it is marked M.O.S. As an aside, I would like to mention the initials M.O.S. For years that I know of there has been a controversy about what they stand for. I am going to tell you those which I have heard, from the ridiculous to the sublime, and let you figure it out. Some film people say it originated when a Hollywood director in the early days called for a scene without dialogue. It seems, so they say, he was of German origin. He would call for the slate to be marked "Mit oudt szound." Another version of the initials is that in the early days the film editors asked for the marking "Motion omit sound." So when the editor saw the slate for the scene he knew there was no sound to be considered. Now the third and last one that I heard is this esoteric version. It is a carry-over from Shakespearean theater for actors who were "Mute on stage." You can take your choice. I do not know.

The slate is used on all filmed productions. That includes major feature films on down. The slate, as I have said, is for the editor. On any filmed action it is there. The example I gave of the scene for a commercial may be a bit extreme. The director will let you walk out from under the lights so that you do not get too hot. If he forgets, then you can step out from under them. You do not have to go far, just from under them.

We have gone through the different types of shootings that you will face in the film industry. The differences are not obvious to the untrained eye. The filmed television show has demands on the set from the actor that are different from those of the taped show. Both of those are different for the actor compared to the commercial. You still act, in all three phases of the film industry. But the manner in which you apply the talent that you have varies from one to the other. Your construction of character, your sensory responses, and your labels are all applied. One application is in a scene that is out of context from the story; the other is in context of the story from beginning to·end. The last is not a story per se, but a message.

These different applications you will find in the film industry outside of Hollywood as well as in Hollywood. Any place in the world that film is shot, it is shot with those demands.

To the actor, when the director calls for "Sound," the reply "Speed," "Camera," the reply "Rolling," "Slate It," "Action," the demands are going to be the same. Then you control the voice and the body. Hence, with these tools, you will work anywhere in the world in the film industry.

An actor must be more aware of the physical senses and the moods than the average person. And he must be able to display them on command even if he really does not feel them. If he is good, then he can convince an audience that he is really experiencing that which the scene calls for.

I hope I have shown the difference in demands between stage and film. I also hope I have demonstrated the way in which you can develop a control over those differences.

COMMERCIAL PLAYERS
1. Print your name.
2. Print agent's name
3. Circle applicable interview

EXHIBIT E
SCREEN ACTORS GUILD
COMMERCIAL AUDITION REPORT FORM

AUDITION DATE _______________

CASTING REP. _______________ COMMERCIAL TITLE _______________

ADVERTISER _______________ PRODUCT _______________ JOB # _______________

ADV. AGENCY _______________ CITY _______________ PRODUCTION CO. _______________

PLAYER'S NAME (PRINT)	SOCIAL SECURITY #	(PRINT) AGENT	PLAYER'S ACTUAL CALL	PLAYER'S TIME IN	PLAYER'S TIME OUT	PLAYER'S INITIALS	CIRCLE INTERVIEW #
							1st 2nd 3rd 4th
							1st 2nd 3rd 4th
							1st 2nd 3rd 4th
							1st 2nd 3rd 4th
							1st 2nd 3rd 4th
							1st 2nd 3rd 4th
							1st 2nd 3rd 4th
							1st 2nd 3rd 4th
							1st 2nd 3rd 4th
							1st 2nd 3rd 4th
							1st 2nd 3rd 4th
							1st 2nd 3rd 4th
							1st 2nd 3rd 4th
							1st 2nd 3rd 4th
							1st 2nd 3rd 4th
							1st 2nd 3rd 4th
							1st 2nd 3rd 4th
							1st 2nd 3rd 4th
							1st 2nd 3rd 4th
							1st 2nd 3rd 4th
							1st 2nd 3rd 4th
							1st 2nd 3rd 4th
							1st 2nd 3rd 4th
							1st 2nd 3rd 4th
							1st 2nd 3rd 4th
							1st 2nd 3rd 4th
							1st 2nd 3rd 4th
							1st 2nd 3rd 4th
							1st 2nd 3rd 4th
							1st 2nd 3rd 4th
							1st 2nd 3rd 4th

PRODUCER
1. Complete top half of form.
2. Sign your name.
3. Mail white copy to SAG on 1st and 15th of each month.
4. Designate person to whom correspondence concerning this form shall be sent _______________

SIGNATURE OF AUTHORIZED REPRESENTATIVE _______________

This commercial audition report is at all commercial auditions. The actor must sign in when he or she reports for the audition. It is a S.A.G. rule.

STANDARD SCREEN ACTORS GUILD EMPLOYMENT
CONTRACT FOR TELEVISION COMMERCIALS

Date___________________, 19_____

Between__________________________________, Producer, and__________________________________, Player.

Producer engages Player and Player agrees to perform services for Producer in television commercials as follows:

Date of Engagement____

Time and Place of Engagement____________________________________

For_______________________________and_______________________________
      (Advertising Agency)   (Advertiser)

Address_______________________________

PRODUCT_______________________________

NO. OF COMMERCIALS_______________________________

Check if Applicable:
- ☐ Dealer Commercial(s)
  - ☐ Type A
  - ☐ Type B
- ☐ Seasonal Commercial(s)
- ☐ Test Market Commercial(s)
- ☐ Non-Air Commercial(s)

CLASSIFICATION: ( ) On Camera   ( ) Off Camera

( ) Player   ( ) Singer-solo or duo   ( ) Singer-Signature-solo or duo
( ) Stunt Player   ( ) Group-3-5   ( ) Group-Signature-3-5
( ) Puppeteer   ( ) Group-6-8   ( ) Group-Signature-6-8
( ) Specialty Act ( ) Group-9 or more   ( ) Group-Signature-9 or more
                  ( ) Contractor   ( ) Pilot

                      Session Fee   Session Fee
                 (On-Camera Players)   (Off-Camera Players)

Compensation: ___________________   ___________________

Check if: Flight Insurance ($10) Payable ☐ $___________
        Wardrobe to be furnished by Producer ☐ by Player ☐
        If furnished by Player, No. of Garments________;
        Non-evening wear @ $5.00 ______;
        Evening wear @ $10.00______;   Total Wardrobe Fee $___________

The standard provisions printed on the reverse side hereof are a part of this contract. If this contract provides for compensation at minimum SAG scale, no addition, changes or alterations may be made in this form other than those which are more favorable to the Player than herein provided.

If this contract provides for compensation above minimum SAG scale, additions may be agreed to between Producer and Player which do not conflict with the provisions of the SAG Commercials Contract; provided that such additional provisions are separately set forth under "Special Provisions" hereof and signed by the Player.

Until Player shall otherwise direct in writing, Player authorizes Producer to make all payments to which Player may be entitled hereunder as follows:

☐ To Player at_______________________________
              (Address)

☐ To Player c/o_______________________at_______________________________
                                (Address)

All notices to Player shall be sent to the address designated above for payments and, if Player desires, to one other address as follows:

To_______________________at_______________________________
  (Name)   (Address)

All notices to Producer shall be addressed as follows:

To Producer at_______________________________
             (Address)

This contract is subject to all of the terms and conditions of the SAG Commercials Contract.

Producer_______________________   Player_______________________

By_______________________

Player hereby certifies that he is 21 years of age or over. (If under 21 years of age this contract must be signed below by a parent or guardian.)

I, the undersigned, hereby state that I am the_______________________ of the above
                            (Mother, Father, Guardian)

named Player and do hereby consent and give my permission to this agreement.

____
      (Signature of Parent or Guardian)

Special Provisions:

Player acknowledges that he has read all the terms and conditions in the Special Provisions section above and hereby agrees thereto.

Player_______________________ Social Security Number_______________________

(W-4 form is attached here.)

Example of a Screen Actors Guild commercial contract.

EXHIBIT "A"

**STANDARD AFTRA EMPLOYMENT
CONTRACT FOR TELEVISION COMMERCIALS
(EXCLUDING EXTRAS)**

Date_____________ , 19____

Between_________________________ ,Producer, and_________________________ , Performer.

Producer engages Performer and Performer agrees to perform services for Producer in television commercials as follows:

____

Date of Engagement ____

Time and Place of Engagement ________________________________

For ____________________ and ________________________________
    (Advertising Agency)   (Advertiser)

Address ____

PRODUCT ____________________ NO. OF
COMMERCIALS ____________

Check if Applicable:
☐ Dealer Commercial(s)
☐ Type A
☐ Type B
☐ Seasonal Commercial(s)
☐ Test Market Commercial(s)
☐ "Non Air" Commercial(s)

Commercial ID_________ ______________ ________

  ☐ Performer does not consent to the use of performer's services in commercials made hereunder as dealer commercials payable at dealer commercial rates.

  ☐ Performer does not consent to the use of performer's services in commercials made hereunder on a simulcast.

CLASSIFICATION: ( ) On Camera   ( ) Off Camera

( ) Actor	( ) Singer or Dancer-solo or duo	( ) Singer-Signature-solo or duo
( ) Announcer (Commercial)	( ) Group-3-5	( ) Group-Signature-3-5
( ) Announcer (Program opening and	( ) Group-6-8	( ) Group-Signature-6-8
( ) closing, standard lead-ins & lead-outs)	( ) Group-9 or more	( ) Group-Signature-9 or more
( ) Stunt Performer	( ) Contractor	( ) Pilot
( ) Puppeteer		
( ) Specialty Act		

                       Session Fee   Session Fee
                 (On-Camera Performers)   (Off-Camera Performers)

Compensation: ____________________   ____________________

Check if: Flight Insurance ($10) Payable ☐ $____________
               Wardrobe to be furnished by Producer ☐ by Performer ☐
               If furnished by Performer, No. of Garments
               Non-Evening Wear@$7.50 _________
               Evening Wear @ $15.00 __________   Total Wardrobe Fee $____________

The standard provisions printed on the reverse side hereof are a part of this contract. If this contract provides for compensation at minimum AFTRA scale, no addition, changes or alterations may be made in this form other than those which are more favorable to the performer than herein provided.

If this contract provides for compensation above minimum AFTRA scale, additions may be agreed to between Producer and performer which do not conflict with the provisions of the AFTRA TV Recorded Commercials Contract; provided that such additional provisions are separately set forth under "Special Provisions" hereof and signed by the performer.

Performer authorizes Producer to make all payments to which Performer may be entitled hereunder by check payable to Performer and sent to the AFTRA office nearest the city in which the commercial was made.

This contract is subject to all of the terms and conditions of the AFTRA TV Recorded Commercials Contract.

Producer__________________________ Performer __________________________

By____

Performer hereby certifies that Performer is 18 years of age or over. (If under 18 years of age this contract must be signed below by a parent or guardian.)

I, the undersigned, hereby state that I am the _________________________________ of the above
                                                (Parent or Guardian)
named Performer and do hereby consent and give my permission to this agreement.

                            ____
                            (Signature of Parent or Guardian)

Special Provisions:

Performer acknowledges that Performer has read all the terms and conditions in the Special Provisions section above and hereby agrees thereto.

Performer_________________________________ Social Security Number_______________
(W-4 form is attached here).

Example of an A.F.T.R.A. commercial contract.

EMPLOYMENT OF DAY PLAYER

Company______________________   Date________________________

Date Employment Starts__________   Name________________________

Part__________________________   Address______________________

Production Title________________   Telephone No.________________

Production Number______________   Social Security No.____________

Daily Rate____________________   Legal Resident of What State______

Weekly Conversion Rate__________   Citizen of U.S.________________

Married______________________   Quota No.____________________

Date of Birth__________________   Date of Entry U.S.____________

The employment is subject to all of the provisions and conditions applicable to the employment of DAY PLAYERS contained or provided for in the Producer-Screen Actors Guild Codified Basic Agreement of 1967 as the same may be supplemented and/or amended.

The Player (does) (does not) hereby authorize the Producer to deduct from the compensation hereinabove specified an amount equal to _____________ per cent of each installment of compensation due the Player hereunder, and to pay the amount so deducted to the Motion Picture and Television Relief Fund of America, Inc.

PRODUCER______________________   PLAYER______________________

By__________________________

Example of S.A.G. day player contract.

THE ARTIST MAY NOT WAIVE ANY PROVISION OF THIS CONTRACT WITHOUT THE WRITTEN CONSENT OF SCREEN ACTORS GUILD, INC.

SCREEN ACTORS GUILD, INC. MINIMUM FREE LANCE CONTRACT

**Continuous Employment - Weekly Basis - Weekly Salary
One Week Minimum Employment**

THIS AGREEMENT, made this........................day of.................. ...., 19........, between

...., hereinafter called "Producer", and

...., hereinafter called "Player".

WITNESSETH:

1. PHOTOPLAY, ROLE, SALARY, AND GUARANTEE. Producer hereby engages Player to render

services as such in the role of.., in a photoplay, the working

title of which is now.., at the

salary of $.. ($....................) per week.
Player accepts such engagement upon the terms herein specified. Producer guarantees that it will furnish

Player not less than..week's employment (if this blank is not filled in, the guarantee

shall be one week).

2. TERM. The term of employment hereunder shall begin on ....

on or about*.., and shall continue thereafter until the completion
of the photography and recordation of said role.

3. BASIC CONTRACT. All provisions of the collective bargaining agreement between Screen Actors
Guild, Inc. and Producer, relating to theatrical motion pictures, which are applicable to the employment of the
Player hereunder, shall be deemed incorporated herein.

4. PLAYER'S ADDRESS. All notices which the Producer is required or may desire to give to the Player

may be given either by mailing the same addressed to the Player at..,
or such notice may be given to the Player personally, either orally or in writing.

5. PLAYER'S TELEPHONE. The Player must keep the Producer's casting office or the assistant director
of said photoplay advised as to where the Player may be reached by telephone without unreasonable delay.

The current telephone number of the Player is..

6. MOTION PICTURE AND TELEVISION RELIEF FUND. The Player (does) (does not) hereby

authorize the Producer to deduct from the compensation hereinabove specified an amount equal to____________
per cent of each installment of compensation due the Player hereunder, and to pay the amount so deducted to
the Motion Picture and Television Relief Fund of America, Inc.

7. FURNISHING OF WARDROBE. The (Producer) (Player) agrees to furnish all modern wardrobe and
wearing apparel reasonably necessary for the portrayal of said role; it being agreed, however, that should so-
called "character" or "period" costumes be required, the Producer shall supply the same.

8. ARBITRATION OF DISPUTES. Should any dispute or controversy arise between the parties hereto with
reference to this contract, or the employment herein provided for, such dispute or controversy shall be settled
and determined by conciliation and arbitration in accordance with the conciliation and arbitration provisions of
the collective bargaining agreement between the Producer and Screen Actors Guild relating to theatrical motion
pictures, and such provisions are hereby referred to and by such reference incorporated herein and made a part
of this Agreement with the same effect as though the same were set forth herein in detail.

9. NEXT STARTING DATE. The starting date of Player's next engagement is____________________

10. The Player may not waive any provision of this contract without the written consent of Screen Actors
Guild, Inc.

11. Producer makes the material representation that either it is presently a signatory to the Screen Actors
Guild collective bargaining agreement covering the employment contracted for herein, or, that the above-referred-
to photoplay is covered by such collective bargaining agreement under the provisions of Section 24 of the General
Provisions of the Producer-Screen Actors Guild Codified Basic Agreement of 1967.

IN WITNESS WHEREOF, the parties have executed this agreement on the day and year first above
written.

PRODUCER________________________   PLAYER________________________________

BY________________________________   Social Security Number__________________

*The "on or about" clause may only be used when the contract is delivered to the Player at least seven days before
the starting date. See Codified Basic Agreement of 1967, Schedule B, Section 4; Schedule C, Section 4; otherwise
a specific starting date must be stated.

Example of S.A.G. weekly contract.

STANDARD SCREEN ACTORS GUILD EMPLOYMENT CONTRACT
FOR INDUSTRIAL—EDUCATIONAL FILMS

THIS AGREEMENT made this _______________ day of _______________________ , 19 _______ , between

_______________________________________ (Producer) and _______________________________________

(Player), shall cover employment in the Industrial-Educational film tentatively entited, _______________

_______________________________________ to be produced on behalf of _______________________________ .

Player, whose home address is _______________________________________ and whose

telephone number is _______________ , shall portray the role of_______________________________ .

The term of player's employment shall be for a period commencing _______________________ and ending
(Starting Date)

_______________________ .

Player shall be employed in the following category:

On Camera Day Player   (   )   On Camera Narrator   (   )
On Camera Weekly Player (   )   Off Camera Day Player   (   )

Compensation: The Producer shall pay to the player: $ _______________ (On Camera Day Player)

$ _______________ (On Camera Weekly Player)

The Producer shall pay to the On Camera Narrator or the Off Camera Day Player:

For the first ten minute unit of finished footage $_______________ ;

For each additional ten minute unit of finished footage $_______________ .

Additional Compensation for Television, Theatrical and Supplemental Exhibition: Producer may acquire the following rights upon payment of an additional 100% of player's total applicable salary provided such payment is made at time of employment or within 90 days of _______________ (first shooting date of production) whichever is later.

    i. Unlimited runs on non-network television
    ii. Unlimited theatrical exhibition
    iii. Exhibition of motion pictures of 7 minutes or less in running time at point of sale or in coliseums, railroad stations, air terminals or bus depots
    iv. Unlimited television exhibition rights outside of the U.S. and Canada.

In the event Producer fails to make advance payment as provided above, producer may acquire such rights thereafter only by separate negotiation and agreement by player subject to the minimums established in Section 6C of the Producers-Screen Actors Guild Mememorandum Agreement of 1974—Industrial and Educational.

Network Television: See Section 6D of the Producers-Screen Actors Guild Memorandum Agreement of 1974—Industrial and Educational.

Distribution of the General Public: See Section 6E of the Producers-Screens Actors Guild Memorandum Agreement of 1974—Industrial and Educational.

Pictures for Government Service: See Section 8 of the Producers-Screen Actors Guild Memorandum Agreement of 1974—Industrial and Educational.

Wardrobe: Check if wardrobe is to be furnished by Player (   ). The number of outfits to be provided is _______ (wardrobe fee for each two day period $5.00 per outfit; dress costume $7.50 for each outfit.)

Special Provisions:

General: All terms and conditions of the Producers-Screen Actors Guild Codified Basic Agreement of 1967 as amended, supplemented or codified, and the Screen Actors Guild 1971 Industrial Agreement and the Producers-Screen Actors Guild Memorandum Agreement of 1974—Industrial/Educational as amended, supplemented or codified are incorporated herein by reference. Player's employment shall be subject to all such terms and conditions.

Producer _______________________________________   Player _______________________________________

By _______________________________________   Soc. Sec. No. _______________________________________
Name and Title

Example of S.A.G. Industrial-Educational film contract.

(Standard AFTRA Engagement Contract, continued)

STANDARD AFTRA ENGAGEMENT CONTRACT FOR SINGLE TELEVISION BROADCAST AND FOR MULTIPLE TELEVISION BROADCASTS WITHIN ONE CALENDAR WEEK

Dated:　　　　197__

Between

hereinafter called "Performer",

and

....

...., hereinafter called "Producer".

Performer shall render artistic services in connection with the rehearsal and broadcast of the program(s) designated below and preparation in connection with the part or parts to be played:

TITLE OF PROGRAM: ....

TYPE OF PROGRAM: Sustaining (　) Commercial (　) Closed Circuit (　)

SPONSOR (if commercial): ....

NUMBER of GUARANTEED DAYS OF EMPLOYMENT: ....
　(if Par. 19 of the AFTRA Code is applicable)

PLACE OF PERFORMANCE*: ....

SCHEDULED FINAL PERFORMANCE DAY:...

AFTRA CLASSIFICATION: ....

PART(S) TO BE PLAYED: ....

COMPENSATION: ....

MAXIMUM REHEARSAL HOURS INCLUDED IN ABOVE COMPENSATION: ....
　(if Par. 56(b) of the AFTRA Code is applicable)

Execution of this agreement signifies acceptance by Producer and Performer of all of the above terms and conditions and those on the reverse hereof and attached hereto, if any.

(PRODUCER)

....　　By ....
　　　　　Performer

....
　　Telephone Number

....
　　Social Security Number

Note: Attach rehearsal schedule or deliver to Performer not later than the first reading session, (or in the event of no reading session, not later than twenty-four (24) hours in advance of the first rehearsal session).

*Subject to change in accordance with AFTRA Code.

(31)

Example of A.F.T.R.A. contract.

DECLARATION REGARDING INCOME TAX WITHHOLDING

I____ declare:
(Your Name)

1. That____ is the only employer for whom I am

working during the calendar week commencing on_______________, 1974.

2. That should I hereafter secure additional employment for wages during said calendar week,
I will notify the above named employer of said fact within ten (10)days after beginning of said additional employment.

3. That it is my desire to have my state and federal income taxes withheld on a weekly rather
than daily schedule pursuant to Internal Revenue Service Tax Regulation Section 31.3402(b)
-(1) (d) (2).

I swear under penalty of perjury that the foregoing is true and correct.

Dated:_______________________________________

____
Signature

*Filling out this form on any job lasting less than a week can save you
a great deal of money by reducing the amount of taxes taken from
your check.*

10

A Summary of Film Acting

It is because Hollywood in the past has set the standard for the film industry, and in the present maintains it, that a Hollywood actor is so widely acknowledged. The term *Hollywood actor* in reality means *film actor*. We have all heard the phrase "star of stage, screen, and radio." That distinction has been around for years. The difference among the three has been known for years by people within the industry and outside the industry. And yet actors have come to Hollywood and have not prepared for the screen. They have simply assumed that acting is acting. I hope that in this book I have shown that it is not.

It is important to you, the reader, that you understand the difference. The theory behind the technique is what will make you function efficiently and convincingly in front of the camera. And that is the point of all this.

I never intended in this book to stir up a controversy about how much more skill it takes to be a film actor than stage or vice versa. What I intended to do is show the demands an actor will face when he gets in front of a camera. Once an actor realizes what will be expected of him, he then can prepare for it. If the actor does not prepare, then his performance is that much less convincing.

The exercises that are described in this book are designed to make the actor or novice familiar with the different areas in which the various roles will take him. You will be angry and violent in one scene and loving and understanding in

163

another. And all within a few hours time and sometimes all within one scene. When you are called upon to perform in these labels, you will do it naturally if you have done it before. It will be conscious choices that you make. And yet your movements will be natural and convincing, and the practice of these is very important. Once you have achieved the point where you can perform in any of the labels and physical senses at a moment's notice, you will understand why it is necessary to keep your mind aware of these labels and your body in condition to perform them. You will find that performing a play in context from beginning to end becomes a privilege. But after having practiced in the exercises you find it easier and easier to get into your labels and choices.

Whatever exercise you feel uncomfortable in, that one you pay attention to. Work on it more often. Do not stay with it exclusively. You will build obstacles that will actually prevent you from solving the problem. So clear your mind of that exercise and go on to another. But then after a while come back and try again.

The exercises all lead up the scene work. It is all directed toward your being able to function on the set with whatever is thrown at you. But still you must be able to work with others. If you can find kindred spirits to practice with, that is excellent. The scenes would be done with each actor contributing his or her performance, but not depending on the performance of the others.

The exercises would have to be performed first for the other actors, the rating system used to evaluate the effectiveness of the actor on set. Each actor in turn would perform the exercise on which he feels he need work. One actor will become the director. He calls "Action" and "Cut." This is done with each exercise. It is very important that they begin and end under those conditions.

If you can get a group together that wishes to gather for the benefit of working out under film conditions, there are some suggestions I have that will add to your skill.

For the exercises, you would write on a piece of paper the different labels. Fold the paper so as not to see what is written. Each member of the group then chooses two slips of paper. After each has had some time to get into the labels he has picked, he hands his slip to the designated director. And then he performs within those labels and the exercise dialogue. The others would then slate the opening and closing label. The director then acknowledges. The director would call "Action" and "Cut."

After those practice sessions have been fairly well controlled, you would go on by putting two people to work on set under the labels chosen.

To accomplish this the group would take six or eight lines from a book or a script. They would number them: one, two, one, two, one, two. Each actor in the group would then be given a number: one or two. The ones speak those lines numbered one, and the twos speak the number twos.

The number ones would then be given the opening and closing label, as would the number twos. They are not to speak about how they are going to perform. The designated director then arbitrarily chooses a number one and number two to perform together. He calls "Action" and "Cut." The other members of the group will rate the opening and closing label of each performer. They will also rate the energy level.

The group can then expand on those scenes by placing additional demands on the actors. The physical senses are added to the scene, as is an economic level. Each time there is a demand added to the scene, both to number one and to number two. When the group begins to get comfortable in those scenes, then they make the scenes longer. Each performer is rated on how convincing he is within the demands of the scene.

If the group decides to work on commercials, then the important element would be time. The dialogue or the action would have to be timed. The call for "Action" and for "Cut" would be between the previously stated time limit—twenty, thirty, or sixty seconds.

The direct on-camera pitch, or the action demonstration of some imaginary product, would be performed just as in the practice scenes. The rating from the group would be the same. The call from the director for "Action" and "Cut" would be the same. The time limit would be the only difference.

For the group to practice cold reading and auditions, the procedure would vary slightly from the scenes. Here each actor would acquire some dialogue from a scene or a commercial or any other source. When the group is gathered, each actor in turn would take the place of the producer or casting director. He would go before the group and state what he or she is looking for at this particular time, and then lay out the demands and audition the group one by one, in front of the group. He would produce the dialogue only after he begins the audition. He presents the demands at the time of the reading.

At these cold reading practice sessions each actor who takes the role of the casting director should have something specific in mind when he auditions. The best thing to look for is whatever he is weak in himself. He chooses the dialogue from that point. Wherever he has been rated low on the scene critique (such as the label, physical sense, economic level, the reading, or the timing in a commercial pitch) is where he can find some solutions to his own problem by assigning that to whoever is auditioning. Then he sits back and watches how the demands were solved. The group will rate the auditions also. The ratings are compared after each audition. That part can vary since it is not necessary to abide by these rules that I have stated here. All I am trying to show is a format that you follow only generally. A group gathering such as this can be very rewarding and a great deal of fun. They are not absolutely essential to you, for obtaining proficiency in the tools of the trade. You can rehearse them by yourself. But if you can get a group together, it is helpful in scene work.

The voice and delivery practice that you will do, you can do alone. The important thing there is that you give yourself a great deal of range. Each day you speak out loud—to yourself, to the walls, to the ceiling, or to any object you choose. The dialogue, as I said, should go from Shakespeare to newspaper ads.

Practice with a tape recorder. Time yourself. And whenever you speak to a microphone, make it convincing. Convince that microphone of whatever you are trying to sell or say at that time.

The film industry has demands that were developed in Hollywood over the years. These demands are as valid in Rome as they are in Chicago or Hollywood. The demands are those of performing before a camera. The key word is not *performing*. It is *camera*. If a film is being shot in the Midwest, it is being shot with a camera. It is a film. The fact that it is the Midwest means nothing to the camera. It will record a performance just the same. The actor on the film can give a stage performance or a film performance. If he applies the technique of Hollywood, and the approach of Hollywood, he will give a Hollywood performance—that is to say, a film actor's performance. Be able to perform a given label at a moment's notice, and do it naturally.

Remember, when you are doing a long shot, you can afford to be broad, and as the camera gets closer to you, you bring it down. The rule of thumb is: long shot, broad; medium shot, cut in half; close up, cut in half again! As you practice your labels and sensory responses you will find yourself at ease in them. This will help you to deliver naturally. When you did the exercises broadly it was to find your limit. Take the entire range. Get familiar with it so that any part of that range can be recalled at any time—and be delivered naturally.

In Hollywood one of the more important things that you must do is to become known. Most of the time it is a slow process. You go on your general interviews, and through them meet the casting directors. After you have impressed one of those casting directors enough to give you your first job, you must find a way to have others in the industry see your performance on the screen. Your agent will tell the people that he knows in the industry of the show you are on and when it will run. Your commercial agent will also do a bit of advertising in your behalf to the casting directors and producers of commercials. But there are ways that you can increase exposure to the industry. Some actors swear by it, others do not.

The film industry has periodicals that tell of what is happening around Hollywood: what films are being shot, and where; who is producing and directing; who is doing the casting—all the information pertinent to the industry. They are "trades," meaning the trade papers. There are several in Hollywood. I will not name them. They are easy enough to find when you get in town. When you want to buy one, you simply ask for the trade paper.

In the trade magazines, the actors who have a show coming up will buy space. Then they insert their picture and the information about the show they are on, when it will be shown. In effect they buy advertising space. People in the industry do read the trades, and there is a great deal of exposure. And, of course, there is the old saying "It pays to advertise." But when you do advertise, you pay the bill.

Some other actors will have small postcards printed up, their picture on one side with space for a short message, the other side for name and address. When they have a show coming up they write a short note about it and send it out to the casting directors and directors. The cards have a personal touch. Many actors will send a note to the casting director and the directors of a show they have worked thanking them for the job. The personal touch with the cards is a nice gesture on the part of the actor. As far as the effectiveness is concerned, I really cannot say.

The actors who have worked around the country still having agents in those places will send the cards to them.

It is a good idea to keep a list of the commercial directors and producers for whom you have worked. Many of the producers who do their filming in Hollywood come from other cities. It is a good idea to send them a hand-written note, telling them of your show. By doing this you are keeping yourself in their minds. And the personal touch will undoubtedly impress them. After all, a Hollywood actor sending a personal note to someone, say in Chicago, or St. Louis, is a matter of conversation for whoever gets it. That means they will talk about you. And maybe think about you when they come back to Hollywood to shoot another commercial.

Another source of potential business for you are the producers and stage shows that you have done around the country. They, too, enjoy hearing about what you are doing. But to these people always send a hand-written note. They are the ones who do the hiring. Let them know that you are thinking about them. They, in turn, will probably think about you. If they think about you when the time comes for casting a show, you have accomplished the goal of becoming known.

Several actors that I know out here have developed what they think is an effective way of getting themselves known in Hollywood. They believe that the answer to the problem of becoming a success is to go to the bars and lounges that the producers and directors frequent. By the proximity of their presence they feel that the important people in the industry will think of them at the time of casting.

One particular actor had been sort of "hanging around" for quite some time. The only progress he had made was with the bartender. This began to bother him. So he took it one step further. He arranged with a friend of his to phone him at the bar at a given time. When the call would come in, the hostess would page the actor. He would sit back for a few minutes till his name was called several times. Then, from where he was sitting, he would loudly proclaim his presence. Then strut boldly across the room. When he got to the phone he would speak in loud, clear terms. What do you think he'd say? "No, tell them I'm booked on another show. If they can postpone the shoot for a while, I'll consider it." That is one way of getting attention. He did that at each bar he went to where film industry people were.

For each actor in Hollywood there is a plan, a way to gain the attention of the film industry. No one can say what is right or what is wrong. What works for one actor may be disaster for another.

A few actors have devised a plan of approach to success by pushing themselves onto the more successful actors. With them it is like this. They will work a show or film with some well-known actor or star. From that day on they are personal friends with that star. They use his first name, try to call him at home, spread the word around town how close they are. They will go to casting directors and directors and use the name of the stars to get appointments. The names of directors and producers are not immune to this approach. As a matter of fact, anyone in the film industry who is working is susceptible.

I suppose that in one degree or another we all have made an attempt at those different methods. We will do what other actors are doing to get attention. After all, that is our business, to get attention. So really, I do not know if it is right or wrong. If it works, well, then it is right. If it does not work, then it is wrong.

But if you put some thought to it, you will find that the real way is to impress the casting director in the beginning, and then to impress those for whom you audition.

One resourceful actor could not get his agent to set up an appointment for him with a particular casting director, and he took matters in his own hands. He called the casting director's secretary. He told her that he was his agent, and would like to make an appointment for an audition for a particular show. The secretary told him there was no room on the appointment calendar. The actor then said that a director had told him to call. At that, the secretary put the call through to the casting director. Most people would have panicked at this. But not him. He imitated his agent's voice and carried on! He made the story so convincing that the casting director agreed to see him. What is more, he got the job! Here is a case where the actor used someone's name, a director, and got away with it. The way he described it to me was that even his agent—to this day—was not aware of what happened. When I told him I was going to use the story in this book, he panicked. It was not until I promised not to use his name or the name of the show that he relaxed.

The actor in this case knew that he could impress the casting director if he could just get in to see him. What he did was unethical, to be sure, and I certainly do not recommend it. But the fact remains that he did win the job. The casting people probably would not be too angry now if they found out about it, because he is good in front of that camera. So the casting director was not embarrassed. But if this were done and the talent did not know how to perform in front of the camera, the results would have been disastrous.

That actor created the opportunity to work in front of a camera. But then he had to perform to continue to get work. So the bottom line is to establish your career by being in control of the tools of the trade, so that your talent can be expressed.

The actor's tools are the voice, the emotions, the senses. The knowledge and skill the actor has of the tools removes the fear of the unknown and breeds confidence. Practice keeps those tools in good working order and the actor prepared to work.

Knowledge of the film industry, the who, the what, the when, will help the actor to get the opportunity to work in films.

It takes both of these elements to become a working film actor. One without the other is not enough. And there is one more factor involved, a factor that many say is the single most important factor of the three—good luck. And I agree, but after all, isn't good luck nothing more than preparation meeting opportunity?

Glossary

ACADEMY DIRECTORY: Publication printed twice a year with photos and information on actors.

ACTION: Term used by the director to actors to begin scene.

A.D.: Abbreviation denotes assistant director.

ATTITUDE: Character's view within a scene, affirmative, neutral, or negative.

AUDITION: An interview where an actor performs his choices for a specific role in a film or stage play.

BEAT: A moment's delay.

BILLING: Actor's name appears when credits are displayed.

BOOM OPERATOR: Person handling boom carrying microphone for sound-man.

BREAK-A-LEG: An expression used by one actor to another actor meaning "good luck."

CALL SHEET: All information concerning a day's filming—talent, location, scenes to be shot, etc.

CHOICES: Actions and delivery chosen by performer to display a character.

CLIENT: Refers to the actor when spoken of by the agent; refers to the ad agency when spoken of by commercial production house people.

CLOSEUP: Camera focuses close on an object or actor.

COLD READING: Delivery of dialogue by an actor without the benefit of time to study the dialogue and make choices.

CUT: Term used by director to actors, camera, and sound man to stop the scene.

DOLLY: A movable cart on which camera is secured for filming.

DUBBING: Dialogue delivered for a film after the film has been made, not necessarily by the actor in the film.

E.C.U.: Abbreviation for "extreme closeup."

EDITING: Arranging the sequence of filmed scenes.

FIRST CARD: Prominant display of actor's name on the list of credits.

FIRST REFUSAL: An option taken by a production company on an actor's time.

FIRST TEAM: Performers on the set.

FLOOR DIRECTOR: (T.V.) Equivalent of A.D. in films. Relays director's orders to cast and crew.

HOLD (put a hold on it): Print scene, uncertain if it is good or not.

HONEYWAGON: Portable toilet trailers used on locations.

INDUSTRIAL FILM: A film shot for use within a particular industry or occupation.

INSERTS: Pickups placed into a master scene.

LINE READINGS: Speaking of lines of dialogue by the actor for the director, but not acted out.

LOCATION: Any place filming is done outside of the studio.

LOOPING: Dialogue of actor in film added to film at a sound studio by the actor.

LOT: The area around the studio.

MARK IT: Call for slate to be clapped and scene to be identified prior to filming.

MARKS: Term used in blocking scenes. Actor begins and ends at certain locations marked out on the set.

MASTER SHOT: An uninterrupted filmed scene or scenes in which pickups or closeups are inserted.

MATCH SCENE: A scene must be repeated exactly.

M.O.S.: When these letters appear on the slate it indicates that there is no sound in this scene.

PICKUPS: Series of shots filmed for insertion into a master scene.

P.O.V.: In script denotes point of view.

PRINT: Scene is good; have film developed and printed.

READINGS: The delivery of dialogue. An audition.

RED LIGHT: Placed outside of sound stages. When lit, filming is in progress; do not enter.

REWRITES: Additional dialogue or rearranged dialogue put into a script or story after final script.

ROLE: A part with a film or stage show.

ROLLING: Response of cameraman to director's call for camera just before action call.

ROUGH CUT: A film shot and edited but not as a finished product.

RUSHES: Film shot and developed of previous day's shooting for viewing by director and producer.

SCENE: A portion of a story for filming or stage presentation.

SCRIPT: A story broken down into scenes with dialogue and direction.

SECOND CARD: Second most prominent display of actor's name on credits.

SECOND TEAM: Stand-in people for actors when crew is setting up shot for lighting, camera angles, etc.

SEPARATE CARD: Actor's name displayed from list of credits.

SOUND STAGE: Specially constructed buildings for filming.

SPEED: Response of sound man to director to indicate recording is ready.

STABLE: Refers to the group of actors all represented by one agent.

STAND-IN: Person hired to take the place of an actor for lighting or positioning or some hazardous action.

STRIKE: To remove from or to dismantle a set.

TAKE: The filming of a performance or scene.

TALENT: Refers to performers.

TOPPING: An actor taking the energy level of one actor and going up from there in voice and delivery.

UP FOR: Used by actors to indicate that they are being considered for a particular role or film.

WARDROBE CALL: The time the talent must appear for wardrobe fitting.

WORK CALL: The time the talent must appear on set.

WRAP: The shooting is completed on a scene or film.

Index